GOOD GOD!
Cry or Credo?

GOOD GOD!
Cry or Credo?

Hubert Black

ABINGDON PRESS
NASHVILLE   NEW YORK

Library of Congress Catalog Card Number: 66-21967

The quotation from Dag Hammarsjköld is from
Markings, tr. by Leif Sjöberg and W. H. Auden,
copyright 1964 by Alfred A. Knopf, Inc. and Faber
& Faber, Ltd.
Quotations from *The Deputy* by Rolf Hochhuth,
tr. by Richard and Clara Winston, copyright © 1964
by Grove Press, Inc.
Scripture quotations unless otherwise noted are from
the Revised Standard Version of the Bible, copy-
righted 1946 and 1952 by the Division of Christian
Education, National Council of Churches, and are
used by permission.

SET UP, PRINTED, AND BOUND BY THE
PARTHENON PRESS, AT NASHVILLE,
TENNESSEE, UNITED STATES OF AMERICA

For CHRISTINE

FOREWORD

This is a book about the biggest question in the world—
the presence of evil and suffering, how we understand
it, and how we cope with it.

Another book about this? The most sensitive spirits
in every age and culture have wrestled with the problem. Is there any more to say? There is always more to
say, for in the end each one of us has to wrestle with
the dark side of life just as if no one had ever done so
before. And each generation has to meet it afresh in the
light of new experience.

What matters is that each attempt to understand, to
offer a guiding light, should be authentic and deeply
personal. We cannot expect to find entirely new and
original thoughts to offer, for we draw on the wisdom
of the past. But such wisdom must have passed through
the crucible of our own dealings with the Enemy and
strike an existential note.

Hubert Black's book has this authenticity. He has read widely and deeply, but this is not a mere distillation. He quotes, but this is no anthology. We have here his own personal key to the problems that are the agony of all who have faith in God. We can sense behind the writing the care of a true pastor as well as the concern of a scholar.

The most striking feature of the book is the clear-cut, resolute decision that *all* suffering is fundamentally evil. There is no tolerance for the view that tragic events are to be accepted as "the will of God," and little sympathy for theories of the educative function of suffering. Not everyone will be able to assent to this radical decision for one side of the age-old debate (there are some awkward texts to be taken into consideration here), but I have the greatest sympathy both for the theological understanding and for the pastoral insight here expressed. It is refreshing to read such an uncompromising statement of the truth that God's will is *good*—without qualification.

Laymen will find that this book speaks directly to the questions every Christian is bound to ask, and ministers will find it forces them to think again and again about their usual answers.

DAVID H. C. READ

PREFACE

The age-old problem of sin and suffering, of tears and death, stares us all in the face, and unless we are to be like children who cover their eyes and pretend that because they cannot see it, it is not there, we have to try for an answer. There are many reasons why I have felt compelled to add my own word to the long debate.

For one reason: I have come across so much "Christian fatalism."

Perhaps this book really started several years ago, in Scotland, when I was going by bus one sunny afternoon into Edinburgh. A little girl, a first-grader, boarded the bus and climbed up on the seat beside me, humming happily. She looked around, asked me my name, asked me which school *I* went to (flattery will get you everywhere!) and then proceeded to entertain the whole bus with a song which I heard that day for the first time. Sweetly she sang,

> Que será, será,
> Whatever will be, will be;
> The future's not ours to see,
> Que será, será,
> What will be will be! [1]

Since then, in many other and older people, I have found an alarming amount of fatalism. There is no such thing as "Christian" fatalism.

Again, I have met so many who were bewildered and torn, not knowing where to turn or what to think—stricken families, broken hearts, clinging to anything for "comfort" even though the comfort was not real. It is very difficult to speak to people in the middle of their agony, for they are too deeply involved; the time when disaster strikes is not the best time to *start* thinking about the origin of suffering and the will of God; that is the time to lean back and rest in a settled and firm belief which is already there in your mind.

Another thing: I have met so many instances of well-meaning friends handing out to people in trouble the most dreadful half-truths about God and his will—distorted, hurtful. Perhaps someone who has told some sufferer firmly and confidently about "this being God's will for you" may take a second thought before blurting out this opinion again. When we look into the tired,

[1] Jay Livingston and Ray Evans.

puzzled faces that ask us "Why?" we should have an answer that is an answer, not a mere dressed-up stoicism; not a noncommittal muttering of pious platitudes accompanied by kindly but feeble pats on the back to keep them quiescent while they fight their lonely way through to a resigned acceptance of the inevitable (called "God's will") in much the same way that they would if they were pagans and had neither church nor ministry to which to turn. An answer that is an answer! necessarily incomplete because man is finite, but real because God is revealed in Christ.

For another: I believe the time is long overdue for the churches to overhaul their formal creeds. No matter how good and careful the formulations were, creeds are the work of men and are fallible. No creed is perfect, and the more detailed and logical and exhaustive it tries to be, the more likely it is to be mistaken. We are now in the time that Bonhoeffer calls, in his famous phrase, the "world-come-of-age"—the day when "Christendom" has gone, when nations no longer feel obliged to call themselves Christian but are frankly and openly secular. This is not wholly loss, for "Christendom" never really existed, and the "Christianity" of nations was a thin veneer on the surface. But even that formal acknowledgment is going, and Christians are being forced to face the fact that they are an ever smaller minority in a world which they are supposed to be winning for Christ; we are not even keeping up, proportionately, with the growth of population. Challenging, reconsidering, and where necessary reforming our creed may be part of the stripping for action which we are going to have to do—and the sooner the better—getting down to fundamentals, asking ourselves, "What is God's will for us in this world-come-of-age? In what ways must our beliefs come of age to match the challenge of the day?"

Some denominations have drawn up modern "statements of faith" which form semiofficial alternatives to their creed or confession. This is largely a waste of time, for if the modern statement says nothing more than the original, it is repetitious; and if it does say something seriously different, it lacks authority. Other denominations have attempted to tone down and amend those statements within the creed or confession which are unacceptable to the modern Christian mind (for example, the doctrine of reprobation and "double predestination"). This is also a waste of time, for the need to tone down occurs in the most "logical" creeds, and just because they are logical you cannot seriously challenge one step without threatening the whole argument. You cannot discard a logical conclusion without imperiling the entire process which led to the conclusion. These are all palliatives. Something more is needed: clear, forthright statements of faith which will give

Christian people a true confidence in facing life and its troubles—and in facing those who say, not as they said to the psalmist, "Where is your God?" but as they more challengingly say to us, "What kind of God?" I hope that this will be an invitation to some to question and rethink.

And finally, I have for long been thinking about this, the basis of our life, and as a result growing firmer in my own understanding of God's good and loving will, reaching a sense of certainty and confidence which I should like to share. This has seemed to come not so much as the result of a search, but rather as light shed on my way.

CONTENTS

That piece of pagan anthropomorphism: the belief that, in order to educate us, God wishes us to suffer. How far from this is the assent to suffering when it strikes us *because* we have obeyed what we have seen to be God's will.

Dag Hammarskjöld, *Markings*

1
THE HARD FACTS
"There are the tears of things . . ."

One day a dear and lovely young girl goes out from
college. She is gay, bright, intelligent, and vivid. She
makes a real and valued contribution, not only to the
life of the school but still more to the friends to whom
she has come to mean so much. But the car skids and
flips—and she is dead. Kind friends, in the spluttering
inadequacy of human sympathy, sit with her dazed parents and pat their hands in a feeble but sincere gesture
of communication; and then, as if to put all things in
perspective, say with a sigh, "Ah well, we must accept
the will of God." Kindness or cruelty?

17

One day a boy grins his gap-toothed grin, waves a hand, and heads for the ball park; and a drunk driver slithers round a corner too fast for control and sideswipes him into eternity—a mangled mass of broken bones, and broken hearts. At the heartrending funeral service a preacher prays, "Lord, thy ways are mysterious and we cannot understand; help us to have faith and accept thine inscrutable will." Affirmation of faith or blasphemy?

One day cancer strikes; one day a plane crashes; one day a foot slips on a ladder; one day a child opens a medicine bottle; one day a father gasps in the sudden pain of a heart attack; one day a mother dies and leaves a young family, as mine did. And through them all the same questions run: how and why and who? God? The devil? Chance? "What then shall we say to this?" cries Paul, facing as every age and every man faces, the same problem of human pain and suffering and the mystery of its origin and meaning. Even as I was writing, I was interrupted by a man who, with much personal trouble in his life, said with tears in his eyes, "Why is there so much evil? Why does God allow it? I feel he has turned his back on me." Nor is he alone in his cry or his tears.

Beyond the personal disasters and tragedies there are the impersonal. An earthquake shatters a city and hundreds, young and old, lie dead in its ruins; a volcano erupts and snuffs out with its hot breath a whole valley,

18

man and beast and leaf; a tidal wave surges in silently from the sea and sweeps its helpless victims away; a hurricane slams into the coast and leaves a swath of destruction and death; an epidemic decimates a whole community, leaving tears and bitterness. Why? The heart of man cries Why? And in his cry there is the note not only of anguish but of anger and bitterness. Why? How? Who? God? Evil? Fate? Nature? Is there any purpose or any meaning? Is there any comfort? What then shall we say to these things?

Only a fool tries to pretend that such things do not face us with a tremendous problem for faith, and that the adequacy or inadequacy of our answer is what will hold us or let us down if and when the testing time comes. One could safely leave out the "if" and just say "when the testing time comes." "It can't happen to *me*" is the old, familiar, and utterly futile cry, for it can and may and often does; and those to whom these things do happen have probably said in their turn, "It can't happen to me"—but it did. Further, the time to question and face up to the problem is *now;* if we wait until trouble comes, we are too deeply in it, too emotionally involved, to see things straight. We need to think ahead and face quietly and seriously the possibility that all we hold dear might be taken from us—and what would we say to such a thing? Or that health and fortune could be

19

snatched away with incredible suddenness—and how would we take it?

We are told by our Lord not to take overanxious thought about tomorrow and its problems, but not to take no thought at all. Our Lord's instruction applies especially to brooding over particular possibilities; you are not to sit and worry yourself sick and silly about what will happen if there is a recession or if the company folds or if arthritis cripples you. You can worry yourself into a decline simply by brooding over particular instances of what might happen; this is what too many people already do all too easily without any further encouragement to gloomy imaginations. It is, however, a very different and wholesome thing to sit quietly and ask yourself about your understanding of the principles involved; about the origin; about the responsibility; and therefore about your own reaction, which will be governed largely by your own view of the basic causes.

Whether you like it or not, you will be forced, by life and its events, to take some view of why things happen and by what agency; that is to say, if you think at all. The only alternative is to be like a cork on a rough sea, thrown now this way, now that, buffeted by life as a helpless and unthinking victim.

Therefore take thought, for here you are deciding what for you are the foundations of life. Your conviction as to the ultimate responsibility for life's events, your view of the cause and effect behind the tragedies and troubles, the disease and grief, will mold your whole attitude to God and man. And no less important, though less often considered, your view of life's happiness and good things will influence your ability to control and enjoy them without reservations, without a clutching fear at the heart that if you are too happy, you will be punished—by something or Someone, God or fate—so that you shiver a little in the warmth of good fortune and cry unhappily in the midst of happiness, as Solon did, "Call no man happy till he dies; he is at best but fortunate."

The aim of this book is to put the questions and stimulate thought and discussion. I shall challenge some conventional answers which I believe to be muddle-headed at best and blasphemous at worst. I can promise no answer for *you,* for your own answer must come from your own heart and head (and which of the two you allow to be uppermost will have some bearing on what answer you reach), and you must decide what you yourself say to these things. There will be more questions than answers. But by the end I shall have given my own answer—the answer that to me is satisfying, that to me is not only logical but loving (for the two unfortunately are not always identical) ; that is to me consistent with Christian faith, that coincides with the New Testament picture of our Lord. You may not agree; I know that many will not agree. Good! Then think it out and come up with something better and truer to the New Testament, nearer to the mind of Christ, and tell *me*. Many will not like it because it disturbs a traditional interpretation and challenges them to new thought and greater responsibility. Good! You need to be disturbed, and so do I.

2

THE CONSTANT QUESTION

". . . and mortal woes touch the heart." VIRGIL'S AENEID

There has been no other question as frequent or as challenging in my ministry. I visit a bright, intelligent woman who is crippled by arthritis, living in constant courage and pain. She has no self-pity, but she has a question and it is, "Why has God taken me out of active life when there was so much for me to do?" What answer or answers can be given? We can say, "Ah, my dear, God's ways are mysterious and beyond our understanding; but someday we shall know and understand and see that it was all for the best." This is the answer so often and so easily given, the answer that seems properly "religious," and from which my soul turns in rebellion, as so often, I believe, the souls of those who hear it, for all their seeming acceptance, turn in rebellion. That they are plainly unsatisfied is shown by the fact that they ask the same question over and over again, *as if it had never been answered.* I believe they are right; it has not been answered by such a reply.

Alternatively we may avoid any direct answer and instead mutter platitudes about patience, faith, and courage, until we make our thankful escape from the presence of something that frightens and dismays us by our inability to come to terms with it in a manner consistent with the greatness of the challenge.

A woman with a young family sees her husband, about to reach the pinnacle of his life's work, have a stroke. Neither bitter nor angry, still she turns to me and says, "Why has God done this to us? I can't understand why he would want to take my husband away from us all—why?" Either you say that he *has* done it, and proceed to explain or justify his act as best you can; or else you deny that it is his act and say (as Jesus said in the parable), "An enemy has done this. God is not an enemy, therefore he has not done it." These are the only answers open to us and a choice has to be made; either God does it or God does not. The third choice—of evading the issue with platitudes

24

—is not a valid choice; it is an intellectual and moral cowardice.

A pastoral counselor tells with proper horror of a child, asking why his daddy had died, being told, "Because God needed him in heaven." As he rightly points out, the result is a sense of bitterness and grievance against God in the child's mind. But no alternative answer is offered—an understandable evasion, as in fact most people in their hearts agree with the basic assumption but do not like it stated in terms of God's "need." Rather they would say that it was God's will to take that man in death, and with that will we must concur. But this, if anything, is a more hurtful thing to tell the child. If God's "needing" his daddy seems harsh to a child who knows how much he himself needs his daddy, at least there is a reason for God's action. But to be told that it is simply an act of God's determinate will and inscrutable power makes God seem a cruel tyrant to the child. How many people there are, young and old, who secretly fear and hate God for what they have been led to believe has been done by him. They do not admit it easily, for they are afraid and ashamed of their feelings, but it shows through the repeated and plaintive question, "Why did he do this to me, to my dear loved one?"

It would seem that the accepted way of counseling those in sorrow is to avoid being definite, to talk vaguely of the goodness of God and of the mystery of his working and of the strange operation of his "love"—a love that takes lover from loved, father from children, baby from mother. We talk around the subject until the bereaved are bemused with words, then leave them to the unsalved wounds from which they will recover in the healing process of time. In hard fact, Christians though we claim to be, we rely more on time than on faith to mend the broken heart. We keep the patient under the spiritual sedation of pain-dulling words until time, the deadener of emotions, has substituted for Christ, the healer of souls.

The centrality of the issue is shown time and again in general literature, where you may often find it dealt with in a refreshingly direct and realistic manner. Sometimes the "secular" gets closer to the problem than the "religious." Every serious novelist and playwright is forced to ask about his characters, the imaginary people from his own brain who act and suffer, think and laugh, love and hate, live and die: What drives them? It is not enough to say that they do it because the will of their author makes them. They must have some reality about their phantom existence if they are to be convincing, and there must be some reason, some cause, evident behind the chronicle of their life and death. Why do they suffer? Why do they endure as they do? What moves them so that they have the power to bring the reader or viewer to sympathy, concern, or even tears? Somewhere, explicit or implicit, there will be a revealing of the author's own approach; a statement of pessimism or optimism, of faith or fatalism.

In the various answers confusion and contradiction reign, which will hardly surprise us when we admit how confused we are in our own minds, and how sharply we differ from one another.

For example, Father Zosimma in *The Brothers Karamazov* says: "Men were born for happiness, and anyone who is completely happy has a right to say 'I am doing God's will on earth.'" But to Job it seems that

> Man is born to trouble
> as the sparks fly upward (Job 5:7)

and Hobbes can say nothing better about the fact, if not the purpose, of life than: "The life of man, solitary, poor, nasty, brutish, and short." For what, then, is man born? What is God's will for him in this life?

Again: What of life's success or failure? Are physical and material benefits really a sign, as many think, of God's blessing and favor? This theme runs through the Psalms—"All that the righteous does shall prosper." We may allegorize and "spiritualize" to some

27

degree, but not to the point where we obscure the unavoidable impression that, in the psalmist's view, virtue leads to worldly gain as well as to spiritual contentment. Remi Nadeau writes of

that unwritten Calvinist doctrine that came out of Colonial New England and spread through nineteenth-century America—the belief that the men of economic achievement were already exhibiting the grace that had put them among the elect destined for heaven.[1]

And the idea is still widely prevalent today in our churches that the good Christian will get on in the world and succeed because God favors him; with the corollary, all too often, that he who has succeeded must be good, for he has been "blessed"; and he who has failed is being punished for his sins. Compare this with Fielding's comment:

There are a set of religious, or rather moral writers, who teach that virtue is the certain road to happiness, and vice to misery, in this world. A very wholesome and comfortable doctrine, and to which we have but one objection, namely, that it is not true.[2]

Is it true that the virtuous "succeed" and the wicked "fail"? And if on a sharper scrutiny we have to admit

[1] Remi Nadeau, *California: The New Society* (New York: David McKay Co., 1963), p. 74.
[2] Henry Fielding, *Tom Jones,* Book 15: chap. 1.

that, on a worldly basis at least, it may be a wholesome and comfortable doctrine but is not true, we may be inclined to ask why? Ought it not to be true, if this is a moral world governed by a righteous power? And if it is not true, what does this say of the guiding principles of life, of the Power that is, if evil is allowed to flourish and grow fat, and good to suffer and be oppressed?

Again: How real is our freedom? Machiavelli, studying the courts and policies of Europe, says: "I hold it to be true that Fortune is the arbiter of one-half of our actions, but that she still leaves us to direct the other half, or perhaps a little less." And Don Quixote, tilting at windmills (which may after all be the more sensible occupation), counters: "I can tell you there is no such thing as Fortune in the world, nor does anything take place there, be it good or bad, brought about by chance, but by the special pre-ordination of heaven." And Melville's Captain Ahab, pacing the deck of his whaler, exclaims: "By heaven, man, we are turned round and round in this world, like yonder windlass, and Fate is the handspike."

So, everywhere, it stares us in the face, the old and daily new problem of our lives: Are we free or bound? Do we will and act, or twitch like puppets on the string? When I choose, do I really choose, or has the choice been made for me—by heredity or fate or the stars or

God? What kind of power is the ultimate in the universe? Is it the little will of man in the vacuum of his own existence in the midst of an uncaring and inanimate universe, or does the world move and life expand under the direction and control of God, who made the heaven and the earth, the sea, and all that is in them? And if so, what God? What kind of God and for what purpose? How far has he made us free and responsible; how far mere puppets? How are we to reconcile the surge of evil, the cruelty and malice, the revolting memories of wars and gas chambers and massacres with the Christian claim of a holy, righteous, loving, omnipotent God and Father? The difficulty of the reconciliation has driven many to a blunt denial of the existence of God. In his chapter on "The Meaning of Providence" Tillich says:

When I spoke to the soldiers between the battles of the last war, they expressed their denial of the Christian message in terms of an attack upon the belief in Providence —an attack which obviously drew its bitterness from fundamental disappointments. After reading a paper written by the great Einstein, in which he challenges the faith in a personal God, I concluded that there was no difference between his feeling and that of the unsophisticated soldiers. The idea of God seemed to be impossible, because the reality of our world seems to be in opposition to the all-mighty power of a wise and righteous God.[3]

And from a vastly different standpoint, Freud, writing of the old but ever-new Oedipus fable, says: "The attempt to reconcile divine omnipotence with human responsibility must, of course, fail, with this material as with any other." [4] Yet Job, through all his suffering, still cries: "I know that my Redeemer lives." Is he just fooling himself?

Does any problem come closer to the heart than this? There are few who have not cried out themselves, "If God is good and just, why, why, why? Why does he allow what happens? Why does he do what he must be assumed to be doing if he is really omnipotent? Why does he not do what is needed to correct and restore justice?" Even if we have never felt compelled to ask this in some hot-and-cold shiver of shaken faith, we have had the experience of some others turning their faces to us, wrinkled with distress and bewilderment, to ask us "Why?" And what then have we said? Have we spluttered an answer that at best was ill-conceived and unconvincing, and at worst was heartless and hurtful? Our helplessness stems from our failure to

[3] Paul Tillich, *The Shaking of the Foundations* (New York: Charles Scribner's Sons, 1948), pp. 104-5.
[4] Sigmund Freud, *The Interpretation of Dreams,* tr. by A. A. Brill (New York: Basic Books, 1955), p. 247.

face the question and drive ourselves to some answer, a failure due to our awareness of the great awkwardness of the question and to the difficulty of the answer.

Inevitably someone will mention the book of Job as if it contained an answer. Job is a fascinating study, in vividly poetic form, of man's condition, and a statement and rejection of various answers to the eternal "Why?" But in the end the book of Job gives no answer to the main question; rather, it answers the question as to man's right to ask the main question; and the answer is *No*. This may be an adequate Old Testament attitude, but it is not an adequate New Testament conclusion. Jesus came to reveal God to us, and we have therefore, in Christian faith and understanding, not only the right but the duty to ask and seek answers which would have been presumptuous in an Old Testament setting. For all its beauty and poignancy, the book of Job gives us all cold comfort, for it offers us no more than the familiar answer of, "No answer— simply submit without question to the unknown and unknowable will of God." For the Christian who faces Christ and hears him say, "If you have seen me, you have seen the Father," this is not enough. There is an answer, and we must each look for it.

Beware the poetic and allegorical in your answer. Beware similes and metaphors. Avoid saying, "It is like . . . ," for it probably is not. The simile will be inadequate and misleading. For example, one simile which claims to "explain" the relationship of God's power and man's freedom compares God to an architect with a great plan, too great for any human mind to comprehend. Everything on the building site looks chaotic as men scurry around doing different, and on the surface unrelated, jobs. But all the time the architect has the great plan, and at last the building is seen —and lo and behold! all the parts fit into place.

We might quote Fielding again and say that "it is a very wholesome doctrine to which we have but one objection, namely, that it is not true." The simile is complete but inaccurate, missing the whole point of the problem. (It is easy to answer a problem if you are allowed in your answer to ignore the problem.) The problem is, of course, that God as the architect lays the plan, and the workmen refuse to carry it out. He says, "Build me a straight wall here," and man says, "No sir! I'll build a crooked wall over there." He says, "Dig a ditch running north and south," and man says, "No sir! I'd rather it went east-west." How then does the plan get completed? This simile assumes that men only *think* they are doing what they want, but are really doing what God wants; that they think they are free, but are actually puppets; and what they count as rebellion against him is in fact, though they do not know it, exactly what he wants them to do. "Rebel" as they may, it is all in the great architect's plan. This is, to me, nonsense, yet it is seriously offered and gladly taken as an "explanation" of predestination, free will, and divine omnipotence. Beware of similes.

The mind rebels against such finagling with the great problem of human freedom and responsibility. Equally the mind rebels against the picture of God as the great puppeteer whose creatures think they are free but are really moving as the divine strings twitch. If all that we do is part of the deliberate plan of God, we are neither free nor responsible; and equally, if all that we do and all that is done to us is part of this plan, then either it is all good (including sin and war and death) or God is not wholly good.

Some are tempted, as Job was, to curse God, for they believe in his existence and in his absolute power, but are unable to reconcile the beastliness of so much of life with the assertion that God is loving and kind. From Prometheus in Aeschylus' play, those long years ago, under the scourge of Zeus and facing his damnation along with the brave and loving Chorus, with the smell of hellfire in his nostrils, crying out against the fickleness and, yes, the evil of the ultimate power as it appeared to him,

> O Earth, O Mother mine
> Most holy, O thou Sky divine,

34

> Whose light is shed on all, ye see
> This anguish and this wrong! [5]

right down to our own day, when the Old Man in
Auschwitz in *The Deputy,* living—if you can call such
existence living—in the stark horror of the Nazi death
camp, with the smell of the burning pits in his nostrils,
cries:

> You terrible God,
> Your Heaven is above us, and the hangmen
> Are men like us, authorized by You.
> Are You watching now? Yes, You will watch.
> Faithfully
> I have always served you among the many who
> Despised you, for I believed in Your omnipotence.
> How can I doubt, Inscrutable One, that
> This too is the operation of Your power! [6]

and in all ages between, men have agonized and questioned, yet all too often have not questioned soon
enough, before agony blunted their edge of thought; or
fully enough, being perhaps afraid of what answer
might come.

When some of the horrors of life face us, we ex-
claim in shocked dismay, "Good God!"

Is he?

[5] *Prometheus Bound,* tr. by Gilbert Murray (London: Allen
& Unwin, 1931), p. 73, lines 1090 ff.
[6] Rolf Hochhuth, *The Deputy,* tr. by Richard and Clara Winston
(New York: Grove Press, 1964), p. 224.

3

THE PURPOSE OF CREATION

"Behold, it was very good." GEN. 1:31

If you should be bold enough to get into the argument in search of an answer, you will find that each question raises another question, and you will be led farther and farther back in man's long story, until you find that you are asking about the very creation of the universe and about God's original will and intention for man and nature. Since the argument leads back step by step to the beginning, let us rather start at the beginning and work step by step forward, in a series of broad statements.

Statement One. The world is, in its origin, God's creation, and was, therefore, in its origin entirely good.

What science tells us of the origin of the universe is vastly different on the surface from the story of Genesis, but there is no real conflict between the two. Nowhere does Genesis claim to be a scientific statement; science, as we know it today, was nonexistent, and the Bible is not a scientific textbook. Genesis is a religious account of the origin of the universe and is not to be taken as a "blow-by-blow" report of literal events; it is a spiritual book conveying spiritual truth. Whether the world was created in six days or in six billion years is, spiritually, unimportant; that however it was created, it was created by God and was therefore wholly good, that it has its origin in his will and is subject to his rule, is important. Suzanne de Dietrich writes:

This world is God's world, brought into being by the breath of his mouth. For this reason, the last word about the world belongs to God and only to God. It is because he is the creator of the world that he is in full control of history, in spite of all appearances to the contrary. Such is the assurance of the prophets. Such is the assurance of the Christian.[1]

"God saw that it was good." In origin, the world was free from all taint of rebellion, and nature was as nature should be, not red in tooth and claw, not striking out

[1] From *God's Unfolding Purpose* by Suzanne de Dietrich, p. 31. Tr. Robert McAfee Brown. Copyright W. L. Jenkins, 1960. The Westminster Press. Used by permission.

viciously with what we blasphemously call "acts of God," but obedient, lovely, kind—the whole creation related to and reflecting the perfect and holy will of the Creator.

Admittedly such a statement annoys more people than it satisfies. To the scientific, it is slightly ridiculous, for it postulates something that cannot be proved; to the fundamentalist, it is more than slightly heretical, for it rejects any literal acceptance of Genesis as the working blueprint of creation. So let us ignore them both for the moment and press on, regardless of complaints, to statement two, which carries the story a stage farther.

Statement Two. God created man in his own image. It would be foolish to pretend that this statement is accepted today as it once was. Jean Wahl's *Short History of Existentialism* expresses the lostness of modern man, without any certainty about his origin or purpose, so often driven from his Christian heritage by the experience of the world's horror, and often repelled from any return by the very people who should be helping him back—by the Christians who attempt to "justify the ways of God to man" in such a way that they are driven farther from him.

In any case the experience of anguish reveals us to ourselves as out in the world, forlorn, without recourse or refuge. Why we are flung into the world, we do not know. This brings us to one of the fundamental assertions of the philosophy of existence: we are without finding any reason for our being; hence, we are existence without essence.[2]

We shall not answer this anguish on the traditional basis of "Behind a frowning Providence, he hides a smiling face," for the question fires right back—"Why the frowning Providence; why the hiding behind it?" It will take something more positive to answer the grim assertion that we are existence without essence.

So let us state again that God made man in his own image. That is to say, he made man good and clean and kind and loving; how else could he be "in the image of God"? As with nature, so man in his origin is good, when "the morning stars sang together and all the sons of God shouted for joy." Now the great majority of us have rejected Genesis as a literal account of creation and are convinced of the basic truth of some form of the evolutionary theory as the most satisfactory explanation, historically and scientifically, of the development of life (though we must remember that science is an evolving process itself and may any day startle us, as it has so often, with some new and still better theory). But if man has emerged from the primitive through gradual development of brain and skill

[2] (New York: Philosophical Library, 1949), p. 13.

39

and conscience, how can this scriptural picture of man created good and humanly perfect be true? Surely the perfect man lies in the far future, not in the distant past; he is still to come, rather than has once been.

We have a contradiction of which there is no resolution. We must reject either the one or the other, or we must admit that there is a paradox and say that somehow, though how we cannot say, they are both true. And so I believe it is. For the inner evidence, the heart and conscience of man, tells us that the Bible is right; man may be scientifically a being on the way up, but spiritually he is a being who has come down. Conscience does not tell us simply that we ought to *become* better, but that we should have been better all along. Conscience testifies to a lost good, to a tarnished gold, to a stained holiness. Somewhere, in our origin, man was made in the image of God. Conscience tells us not that we must learn, but that we once knew and have put the knowledge from us and must relearn.

There is no answer free from some apparent contradiction; the materialist view of man as an emergent being on his way up from the simple to the complex, from the slime to the sublime, fails utterly to explain how conscience, an awareness of what should be, a sense of the challenge to become something higher and better than he has ever in fact known, develops; nor can it explain how mind, imagination, love, sacrifice emerge

40

from slime. We must equally admit the problem in the traditional view of man as a "fallen" creature; there is no record of a Golden Age when man was perfect and all the world was fair. On any religious view of man, as a spiritual being, it is as hard to conceive of a once-perfect man become corrupt as it is to conceive of a moment in time when a mere emerging animal was suddenly endowed with a soul.

I believe the testimony of conscience is to the spiritual and psychological truth of the biblical view of man; the root of man's anguish lies in his sense of something *lost;* and when a man turns to God and receives forgiveness, he has the sense of being *restored,* as to something once held and thrown away. However difficult the doctrine of some "fall" may be, it is less difficult than the alternatives.

Further, I believe that some of the peculiarly acute sense of "predicament" today, of despair beyond mere dismay, is in fact due to the loss of this sense of man as fallen. Modern man's picture of himself as one on the way up but unable to make the grade, who has failed and is failing (and on a reasonable projection is going to continue to fail) to match the demand of his environment and the challenge of his technical potential, leaves him feeling like a child trying to build a model which needs the skill and coordination of an adult—trying to do that of which he is inherently incapable; and because he has no confidence that he will become adequate before it is too late, he knows despair.

The biblical view also sees man as having failed and failing still, but sees him, rather, as an adult who has allowed himself to revert, in a form of infantile regression; the good he seeks and fails to reach, mankind has known; the good he wants is possible, for it was once so; and though he cannot recover it for himself, he knows that the God from whom the good came is urgent to restore it to him, so that, though dismayed, he does not despair. But this is to look ahead; at the moment let us go on to the next statement.

Statement Three. Man is a fallen creature. Now, of course, this statement is not just about man's condition but also about the vital element in his God-given nature which made this fallen condition an inherent possibility, as God knew and accepted. For God did not make man a puppet. He could have done so if he had wished; he could have created perfect men and women in whom the impossibility of revolt against him would have been absolute. If he had wanted to create beings unable to sin, he would have done so. He did not. Instead he made man in his own image, and therefore gave man a freedom, full of glory and of danger. God gave man free will.

And here the battle gets going. Here we get to the meat of the matter, and here we set our general line of thought which will affect our attitude as the question occurs and reoccurs, not only through the Bible, not only through literature, but in our personal daily life. This in some way sets our thought about God, about ourselves, our duty, our responsibility, our relation to our fellowmen. This eventually will help to color our thinking and shape our whole outlook on the world, on men, and things. You name it; this affects it. God made man *free*.

If man had not been free, he could not be described as being in the image of God. God is free to will, to act, to do as he may please; the instant you imply any limitation to him, you cease to think of him as God. Yet there is, in a way, an inner limitation—the inability of the wholly and innately good to do any wrong; whatever is wrong is so abhorrent to him that we can say that he cannot will it. Hegel says: "God is the absolutely perfect being and can therefore will nothing other than himself—his own will." [3] The freedom of God is absolute—the freedom to be himself and execute his holy will. The freedom of man is secondary. It is freedom to obey his creator and to do his creator's will. It is a lesser freedom, but it is a real freedom; and because it is both real and lesser, it has in it the possibility of refusal. If man is free to obey, he is also free to disobey; the one implies the other. Man's good-

[3] Hegel, *Philosophy of History,* Introduction, section 3.

ness is not inherent as is the goodness of God; man's goodness is conditional, dependent on his continued obedience and alignment to the wholly good and innately pure, to God.

And man rebelled. This is not just the testimony of Genesis; it is the testimony of the conscience. "I have sinned" is the admission forced from us. And the seriousness of it is that we have not just "made a mistake" or "been foolish" or "misjudged the situation" or "misunderstood," but that we have, in every sin, sinned against the God who made us for obedience. There is profound spiritual insight in David's cry in Psalm 51, his prayer of repentance after his adultery with Bathsheba, when he says, not "I have sinned against Bathsheba and her husband," but "against thee, thee only, have I sinned, and done that which is evil in thy sight." Sin is against our fellowmen and women, sometimes against our own bodies, but first and foremost it is sin against God who made man in his own image and who looks for obedience; and man is fallen, and we, together and individually, are driven to acknowledge it. Nor can we acknowledge it as a past fact for which we are not directly responsible, but only as a direct and personal fact for which we bear our blame. It is not enough to say "man is fallen"; we cry "I am fallen." In the Genesis story, however unhistorical, we see personal truth; in Adam and Eve

44

we see not just distant and mythical prototypes, but the inner conflict of our own hearts. This is the "anguish of the human heart which can no longer stand the power borne by the daemonic forces on earth" [4] of which Tillich writes. Dr. de Dietrich says: "In reality, what the account reveals to us is the whole tragedy of our situation as men created for life and placed under sentence of death." [5]

God did not create evil any more than you can say that light creates darkness. Dr. de Dietrich notes that "the story of the Fall is not an attempt to explain the origin of evil, for it does not tell us where the serpent came from. It is important to realize that the serpent is a creature, and not an eternal principle co-existent with God." [6] God did not create sin, nor did he ordain that man should sin. If that were so, then he would have contradicted his purpose of creating man in his own image for fellowship with him; and "sin" would not be "sinful" if God ordained it, for all he does is good. The only limitation we can admit in God is that he can do no wrong nor can he create wrong, for it would be a contradiction of his own nature. This is fundamental, but so often ignored; in our later thinking about the specific ills and sorrows of man, this must be at the

---

[4] Tillich, *The Shaking of the Foundations,* p. 105.
[5] De Dietrich, *God's Unfolding Purpose,* p. 37.
[6] *Ibid.*

base of our thinking, that God can will nothing other than the good. Man's sin, then, in its origin and nature is *outside the will of God;* it is a contradiction, a revolt, an offense. Man, by his own misuse of God's gift of freedom, has fallen.

Now this implies some deliberate self-limitation by God. Man cannot be truly free unless God gives him the freedom, and if man is to be free in his origin to accept or reject, then God limits himself in that situation, which is *of his own deliberate choice and will.* Man does not limit God; God limits himself in order that man may be free to live with God in the fellowship of the created with his creator—or free, as in fact has happened, to turn away from him in deadly pride. To talk of God's self-limitation does not, as so many fear, imperil the doctrine of the sovereignty and omnipotence of God. God does not need our fervent arguments for his sovereignty! For it is his omnipotent will that has made man and his freedom, his omnipotence that determines to have this situation in which revolt is an implicit possibility; and it lies utterly within the power of God to abolish the situation and to remove man's freedom. But as long as he wills to let men be free, then that is his omnipotent will.

To this, too, the mind and conscience respond. We may evolve deterministic theories on scientific or religious grounds; we may, as a theory, hold that man's thought and action are determined by heredity or environment or both. But we do not believe it in practice, with regard to our own lives and choices. We may, as a theory, hold that the doctrine of omnipotence cannot allow for any real freedom, but in fact we do not believe it with regard to our own lives. As Samuel Johnson said, when an overlogical doctrine of omnipotence and predestination was put to him, "Sir, we are free, and we know it, and that is an end of it."

Statement Four. Nature has been corrupted along with, or by, man's sin. Nature no longer presents the intended picture of peace and kindness, but is twisted and distorted into something of a caricature of itself. (A speculation here: Is the corruption of nature confined to this planet of man's existence on which man's revolt took place, or has it had a cosmic effect? Is the whole universe tainted by man's rebellion, or only this earth, man's home? If the universe is untouched and moves still in perfect obedience to its creator, what may far future space flights carry with them? We know that elaborate precautions are being planned to insure that germs of disease are not carried out to contaminate the moon or planets; but what of the spiritual disease of man, his corrupting pride, from which the physical diseases take their origin? Will it become an infection even of "dead" stars?)

A sensitivity to the sorrow as well as to the beauty

of nature, to its pain as well as to its joy, is all too rare. We think about "Nature" with the attitudes of an increasingly urban and industrialized society; "Nature" is nice to commune with for refreshment of body and mind. And indeed it is nice and refreshing, but only to a limited extent; "back to Nature" means also back to a cut-and-thrust, survival-of-the-fittest, red-in-tooth-and-claw nature of tremendous and unpredictable power. The sudden onset of fog or a snowstorm on the mountain when seemingly all was fair; the unexpected viciousness of a line squall on the water out of a clear sky; the quiet and horrible sucking-down of quicksand or a whirlpool without warning—there are enough of these, and often enough, to contradict our rosy sentimentalities about "Nature" with a capital "N." It is not true, as W. S. Gilbert sings in "Princess Ida" that "Man is Nature's sole mistake!" Nor is it true that "every prospect pleases and only man is vile," for if Bishop Heber had gone deeper into the life of nature in "Ceylon's spicy isle" (or for that matter in "England's green and pleasant land") he would have found that nature, too, for all its beauty, is "vile." It is a superficial view of nature that leads us to sentimentalize about it, for it overlooks the real problem of nature—a problem that makes itself known to us not only in the obvious challenge of natural catastrophes but in subtler ways, in the faint sense of melancholy and the breath of sadness that touch even our happiest communing with nature; for the sadness is not just for ourselves that we cannot enjoy it fully or forever. The sadness is for nature itself. Typically, when a man penetrates beneath the surface, he is forced to change his view and begins to grow into a deeper sense of a true community with nature; we are one with nature because in some real way nature is one with us in our corrupt existence. Witness the change in Wordsworth's attitude; first:

> For nature then . . .
> To me was all in all.—I cannot paint
> What then I was. The sounding cataract
> Haunted me like a passion: the tall rock,
> The mountain, and the deep and gloomy wood,
> Their colours and their forms, were then to me
> An appetite; a feeling and a love,
> That had no need of a remoter charm,
> By thought supplied, nor any interest
> Unborrowed from the eye.[7]

Then:

> I have learned
> To look on nature, not as in the hour
> Of thoughtless youth; but hearing oftentimes
> The still, sad music of humanity,
> Nor harsh nor grating, though of ample power

[7] "Lines Composed a Few Miles Above Tintern Abbey."

> To chasten and subdue. And I have felt
> A presence that disturbs me with the joy
> Of elevated thoughts; a sense sublime
> Of something far more deeply interfused,
> Whose dwelling is the light of setting suns,
> And the round ocean and the living air,
> And the blue sky, and in the mind of man.[8]

Here is the note of sadness that serious thought on nature always brings. Paul was aware of it and spoke of it when he told us that "The whole creation has been groaning in travail together until now" (Rom. 8:22), and his comment, which seems so strange to many, has touched the hearts of others. It is Gilbert Murray, the professed agnostic, who says:

"The whole creation groaneth and travaileth" says St. Paul. I suppose the vast majority of mankind, as long as they are fairly comfortable themselves, do not realise at all the meaning or the truth of these words. To those who do, the Prometheus seems to be "telling their own dream." [9]

And on the same text Tillich has a moving chapter that takes as its title a quotation from Schelling, "Nature also mourns for a lost good."

Nature is not only glorious; it is also tragic. It is subjected to the laws of finitude and destruction. It is suffer-

[8] *Ibid.*
[9] *Prometheus Bound,* tr. by Murray, Introduction.

ing and sighing with us. No one who has ever listened to the sounds of nature with sympathy can forget their tragic melodies. . . . The melancholy of the leaves falling in autumn, the end of the jubilant life of spring and summer, the quiet death of innumerable beings in the cold air of the approaching winter—all this has grasped and always will grasp the hearts, not only of poets, but of every feeling man and woman. The song of transitoriness sounds through all the nations. . . . The tragedy of nature is bound to the tragedy of man. . . . Man and nature belong together in their created glory, in their tragedy, and in their salvation.[10]

If, then, nature too is fallen and corrupt, we must keep this fact constantly in mind when we think about all natural events. In view of this, to talk of an earthquake as an "act of God" in any serious sense, as meaning that nature is uncorrupted, as meaning that it happens through the obedience of nature to the will and determination of God, is plain nonsense. To say "God's ways are mysterious" when a tidal wave drowns thousands is worse than nonsense; it is a form of blasphemy if it means that nature is a true expression of God's will and moves at his command. This is nature corrupt, as man is corrupt—still subject to God's ultimate control, still a vehicle for God's revelation, but imperfectly so—no longer a mirror but a distorting mirror.

[10] *The Shaking of the Foundations,* pp. 81, 83.

The natural world gives evidence of its involvement in man's rebellion against the creator and against the purpose of creation, which is obedience to God.

By their cruelty and greed, by their disease and violence, man and nature demonstrate their fallen state; for just as man is unhappily aware that he should all along have been other than he is, so nature mourns—not for a good that has never yet been and is to come, but for a lost good, for a good that once was real and enjoyed, and lost.

4

THE REVOLT OF MAN

"I struck the board and cried, No more; I will abroad."
GEORGE HERBERT

Let us take a deep breath before going farther and summarize what has been said so far. The essence of it is that God is good and only good; that all that he has made is good and only good; that anything that is not good is not his creation—either in man or in nature. If man's sin is in any way ordained by God, it is not sin, for God cannot ordain wrong; and if a natural disaster is ordained by God, it is not a disaster —it is a blessing, for God ordains only what is good. If disease and untimely death and bitter loneliness are God's will, then they are good not bad.

"Hold it," someone cries, "that's not fair! Doesn't

God send suffering so that good may come in his mysterious ways?" This is a familiar, well-meaning argument, popular and misguided. It lies back of such a prayer as this, taken from a devotional daily study book: "Enable us patiently to bear whatever thou sendest us to suffer."

Let a little logic play on this idea. "God sends us suffering." This is quite different from saying "God sends his people into a world which, because it is sinful, will make them suffer." Rather, the proposition is that God himself sends suffering, deliberately and purposefully; it is to be found time and again, as, for example, in the well-known hymn verse by Horatius Bonar:

> Take thou my cup, and it
> With joy or sorrow fill
> As best to thee may seem;
> Choose thou my good and ill.

But how can it be "ill" if God chooses it? It can only *seem* to be ill, but in reality must be good, for God does not ordain "ill." The words "God" and "ill" are mutually exclusive. If it is argued that it is really ill but is sent to bless us ultimately, two comments will suffice. The first is that it makes God less moral than a good man, for it defies the principle that the end does not justify the means; we are morally forbidden to use "evil so that good may come"—and will God do less than man? The second is that some people, without realizing it, come close to making God out to be sadistic.

God is good and all that he does is good, and if it is good it is from him. Refer everything to this and test every argument by this. So, with this in mind as a basic rule, let us make our next statement.

Statement Five. Suffering, pain, and death are evil. That is to say, they are contrary to the will of God. Before going any further with this statement, which, as I know from experience, meets with considerable opposition, let us look at what we mean by the phrase "the will of God." We use it often, casually, unthinkingly, without defining in our minds what we mean by it. Of course, if we adopt a deterministic view of the world (on a religious basis) then the phrase "the will of God" presents no difficulties, for everything, including the fall, man's sin and death, are all willed by God and purposed by him for his "great glory." (This seems too absurd to mention, but when carried to their real conclusions, the beliefs of many Christian people fit right here, all too neatly. No wonder such people are constantly appealing to the "mystery of Providence" and the "inscrutability of God!")

Rejecting any deterministic view, religious or scientific, we are driven to ask ourselves what we mean by the "will of God." Do we mean God's original purpose in the creation, when he made all things, including man and nature, pure and good? Or do we mean God's active work in the actual situation of a corrupt world and sinful man—a corruption which is outside his original purpose, his will? Or do we mean his final purpose towards which he moves and no man shall hinder him? [1]

Is it God's *original purpose* that man should suffer and die? Is this what we mean when we say that "we must accept the will of God" when, say, some happy young life is cut short by brutality or stupidity? Is it God's original purpose that some children be born hydrocephalic, that some be born mentally retarded, that some be spastic? If not, why in the name of all that is holy do we say to their parents, "Accept the will of God"? Is it his original purpose that men and women should scream and die, or worse still sometimes, scream and live? In the face of all the pain and suffering of life, can we say "This is God's will" and not be blasphemous?

In God's original purpose, all is good, without pain or death. And as striking confirmation that this is his

[1] Dr. Leslie Weatherhead's book *The Will of God* (Nashville: Abingdon Press, 1944) is a classic treatment. He writes of the "Intentional Will of God," the "Circumstantial Will of God," and the "Ultimate Will of God." Like many others, I am deeply indebted to him for his book.

purpose, we are called to look to a time when this is to be brought about again, when his will is to be finally established, when there will be a new heaven and earth and "death shall be no more, neither shall there be mourning nor crying nor pain any more." But if, as some of our grimmer-minded religious tell us, God sends pain and suffering, how shall they be excluded from the new heaven and earth? If they are inherently good, they will be present in heaven, and there *will* be pain and sorrow and suffering and tears and death, which is absurd. If they are not inherently good, what is the good God doing by using them? Sending evil to promote good?—immoral! Inflicting pain and suffering?—sadistic!

There are two perversions common in some degree in all mankind, and because they are perversions, they are wrong, distorted, evil. The one is sadism, which is the enjoyment of inflicting pain on others; the other is masochism, which is the enjoyment of pain inflicted on oneself. We have to recognize the pervasive power of these perversions and guard not only against the fact of them in our lives but also their invasion of our thinking, even our thinking about God. Many of our common ideas of "God's will" have their root in one or other of these perversions; and still more regrettable, many of our ideas about God himself impute to him the same perversions that infect us. The way some think about man's lot and grief makes God to be sadistic; the way some think about the cross makes him to be masochistic.

It is probably unavoidable that much of our thinking about him should be anthropomorphic—thinking of him in human terms, elevated and enlarged. How else can we think except in terms of our own human experience? So we use words like "Father," "King," "Judge"; and it is inevitable and right, for this is how we understand; Jesus himself uses these terms to convey to us the truth about the Godhead. But we must be alert to avoid "humanizing" God when us use these words, and we must remember that because they spring from our human experience they have different, sometimes vastly different, shades of meaning according to the particular experience of each individual. I remember Professor H. R. Macintosh warning his class about using the word "father" as if that word by itself would be adequate without further definition—reminding us that we would meet men and women for whom the word "father" was a repellent word, bringing at once to their minds a picture of drunkenness, cruelty, neglect, and for whom the word "father" could never have the warmth and color that it has, in varying degree, for most of us. Tell such unfortunates that "God is our Father," and the picture that springs unbidden to their minds is hateful and horrible. Even the best human

father falls so far short that we must beware of thinking of God as simply an enlargement of humanity; far
too easily we carry some of humanity's failings into
the picture, and before we know what we are doing,
we are talking of a "loving Heavenly Father" who
sends his dear children suffering and grief in order
to "make them better."

But what of "punishment"? Is not some suffering
sent by God as punishment, chastisement? The idea is
expressed frequently in the Old Testament and is repeated with seeming approval by Paul in his first letter
to the Corinthians: "Whom the Lord loves, he chastens.
God, the loving Father, punishes and chastises his
children for their own good." There is much to com-
mend the idea, but there are some serious objections
and qualifications to note.

1. If suffering is punishment meted out by God,
why is it meted out so inequitably? True, it was said
of Ignatius Loyola that he punished seemingly most
unfairly those under his command; and the inequity
was explained by the fact that he punished each not
according to the actual severity of the offense but according to the individual character of the offender. So,
it may be argued, God punishes not according to rule
but according to individual circumstances. For all its
plausibility, there remains something repellent—the
idea of great inequity in punishment for similar offenses

is in itself an offense against our God-given sense of justice and fairness.

2. It is dangerously anthropomorphic. A human father, himself imperfect, may punish his child for want of wit or wisdom, grace or understanding to know some better way. Simply to transfer the practice of human chastisement (itself so often a token of failure and inadequacy) to God is perilous. A human parent, however "righteously" or "disinterestedly" he may punish, however much he may say that he does it not in anger but in sorrow, however much he may claim that it hurts him more than it hurts the child and that it is done only to help the child, still feels in some sickened and sickening way touched and tainted by the very thing he tries to eradicate. This is the parental dilemma—not to punish is to condone wrong; to punish is to become involved in wrong. It is a human dilemma from which we cannot escape, but we should be duly hesitant to impute the same dilemma to God. We, who receive and transmit punishment, are part and parcel of the corrupt and sinful world in which sin and punishment exist. God is not.

3. Much human suffering, as we know, cannot be laid directly to the charge of the individual concerned; the baby born blind of syphilitic parents suffers, but not in punishment. To attribute such suffering to God's "chastening" action is to call him vengeful and un-

just. The most that you can say is that *some* suffering *may* be "chastening from the Lord."

4. We must ask further, in what way is it "from the Lord"? What motive do we attribute to God when we talk of him punishing his children? Do we mean to imply that he says "I will punish them for their sins" or "I will save them from their sins even though it may hurt"? There is a very real difference.

The idea that God punishes his children is strikingly absent from the Gospels and is rather contradicted than supported by the whole emphasis of the Gospels. Those who favor the idea have to look elsewhere for support— in particular to the Old Testament. The only direct use of the word for punishment by Jesus occurs in Matt. 25:46, and this refers not to this life but to the life to come. Further, the word used for "punishment" is *kolasis,* which means originally "pruning," and from that "remedial or corrective" treatment. William Barclay writes:

Even the words *eternal* and *everlasting* in Matthew 25:46 are significant. In Greek they are the same word, *aionios.* . . . The only person in the universe who can properly be called *aionios* is God. Therefore it could well be argued that *kolasis aionios,* so far from meaning final condemnation, means remedial punishment such as it befits God to inflict. . . . If God is love, can we conceive of God being satisfied with a universe in which millions of his children

are undergoing punishment for ever and without end? . . .
Could any human father be satisfied when any child of his
was somewhere being endlessly punished? Must not love
still act? Can heaven be heaven while millions of God's
children are in hell? [2]

It is a warm, appealing, and attractive argument. It
suggests a form of Purgatory alien to both Protestant
and Roman Catholic thought. C. S. Lewis, in his fascinating and haunting *The Great Divorce,* writes in
much the same vein in what he calls an "imaginative
supposal"; in it he asks his mentor: "But is there a
real choice after death? My Roman Catholic friends
would be surprised, for to them souls in Purgatory are
already saved. And my Protestant friends would like
it no better, for they'd say that the tree lies as it falls." [3]
Barclay seems to challenge the traditional Protestant in-
sistence on this life as decisive for man's eternal destiny,
while from the Roman Catholic side, Father Teilhard
de Chardin writes:

Of all the mysteries which we have to believe, O Lord,
there is none, without a doubt, which so affronts us as that
of damnation. . . . We could perhaps understand falling
back into inexistence . . . but what are we to make of

[2] William Barclay, article in "Life and Work," the Record of
the Church of Scotland.
[3] C. S. Lewis, *The Great Divorce* (New York: The Macmillan
Company, 1946), p. 65.

eternal uselessness and eternal suffering? You have told me, O God, to believe in hell. But You have forbidden me to hold with absolute certainty that a single man has been damned.[4]

The day is mercifully gone when the church spoke with almost lip-smacking relish about the eternal punishment of the nonelect. I believe we must go farther and must be very careful in talking at all of "punishment" in connection with God's redemptive action. The word is so loaded with human overtones and covers such a wide range of human motives and emotion that it should not be used without careful definition.

If we are to use human analogy, a safer and truer analogy than that of parent punishing child is that suggested by Gregory of Nyssa—the analogy of the surgeon who does what must be done to restore health; but any pain he causes is caused not to "punish" the patient but as an inevitable part of effectively dealing with the disease; that is to say, the pain comes, in its cause and origin, from the disease, not from the healer.

So, too, with the addict going through the agonies of withdrawal from his addiction. The agonies are the direct result of the addiction; they are not given

[4] Pierre Teilhard de Chardin, *The Divine Milieu* (New York: Harper & Row, 1960), p. 129. *Note:* the subject of Universalism, the belief that all will be saved in the end, is commented on in a footnote to Chapter 7.

him by his doctor in "punishment"—they come from within, from the sin. The doctor's sole and only aim is to free the patient from the addiction; this can only be done with pain, but the pain is in its origin due, and due only, to the sin of addiction, not to the curative work of the healer.

So, I submit, with human addiction to sin, from which God offers to set us free; there may be suffering in the process, for we have to give up much that is dear to us, much that has become part of us; but it is *we,* in our common humanity, who have made the suffering. The suffering, like all suffering, is *in its origin* from the sin, not from him who seeks to set us free.

None of us as children believed the old parental story that "this hurts me more than it hurts you." We did not believe it then, and we can scarcely make ourselves believe it now, when we are told that God, the loving Father, hurts us for our own good, but that it hurts him more than it hurts us. I am sure that in a very different way it does hurt him more than it hurts us, but it does so because it is *not* his doing nor his will, and he grieves over us and for us because his purpose for us is peace and joy and love, not pain and grief and death; and his purpose, his will, has been rejected and set aside. God grieves over us because he has so much else in mind and heart for us, and his plan and purpose call for so much that we cannot or will not accept. All the pain and grief and death come from sin; none of it from him. It is not his purpose ever to inflict suffering, not even as "punishment," but only and always to release us from the suffering which we bring on ourselves, directly or as part of our common humanity.

This seems to me so self-evident, so clearly the mind of Christ, that I wonder sometimes why so many people drive themselves to a different picture of God; and I find, in the main, two reasons—one of them theological, the other psychological; and both of them mistaken.

The first is an overemphasis on the sovereignty of God. "The Lord our God the Almighty reigns"; everything is his and "he's got the whole world in his hands." This is the very ground of our confidence, and if we had no certainty of God's power, we should be pitiful creatures indeed. But, in Dr. Weatherhead's words:

The omnipotence of God, you perceive, does not mean that by a sheer exhibition of his superior might God gets his own way. If he did, man's freedom would be an illusion and man's moral development would be made impossible. . . . When we say, then, that God is omnipotent, we do not mean that nothing can happen unless it is God's will (= intention). We mean that nothing can happen which can *finally* defeat him.[5]

[5] Weatherhead, *The Will of God,* chap. 3, p. 33.

This is a real, but for many unseen, distinction. It is felt that it, as it were, "lowers" God to admit that anything can happen contrary to his will, and that to prop up God and his greatness (as if he needed it!) we must somehow squeeze everything that happens into "his will," no matter how distorted, to the point of absurdity, this makes our personal story and world history. It is surely plain in the biblical view of the world and man in creation that God omnipotent decreed that there should be freedom—even freedom to reject him. It is surely plain that God in his omnipotent wisdom still allows man such freedom as may be left to him in his corrupt state. This is the basis of our daily thought and action. This is what we live by; this is what each of us knows and believes deep down, however much we may pretend otherwise on the surface. God's sovereignty needs no propping up by our small hands, nor does he need an overeager assertion of his omnipotence.

The second reason is one of comfort. Many people, struck by life's bitter blows, cannot bear to face them in all their raw cruelty and evil. It is a seeming comfort to say, "This dreadful thing that has happened is really part of God's plan, and someday, somehow, I shall understand why it happened and see the plan and realize that everything was really for the best, even though it seemed hurtful and cruel at the time." One hesitates to undermine anyone's ground of comfort, but it has to be pointed out that by taking this attitude *they are avoiding facing the reality of evil;* and no man is going to progress far in faith and understanding who does not face the terrible reality of evil. They shut their eyes to it, for they cannot bear to look at it, and they pretend that somehow it is all God's work and that it will turn out to be good and right in the end. This may defend the sovereignty of God, but it attacks his holiness by imputing to him the use of wrong that good may come, or else commits the heresy of denying that there is any evil—that it is all a mirage because it all turns out to be the good God's good will in the end.

Moreover, this seeming comfort of believing that all comes from him, even pain and death, is bought at too great a cost. Quite apart from the real attack on his goodness which is implicit in it, there is often great psychological damage. Someone who, say, has lost a loved one says, "This tragedy in my life, bringing dreadful loss and grief, is really his will and I must therefore accept it and believe that someday I shall understand why he did it to me"; and then, deep down in the heart, adds, "And I hate him for it because it is cruel and horrible." There is a tremendous tension built up in those who force themselves to believe that because he is omnipotent, all that happens must be in accord with his will and purpose, for there is a natural inclination to hate One Who Hurts.[6] I have known the realization of what had been going on in the deeps to bring a sudden flood of tears, healing tears, and the frank and horrified admission that under the forced acceptance there had been a real and bitter resentment against God. Suffering and pain are not his will.

Nor is death his will, in the sense of his original intention for mankind. Paul says very plainly that the "wages of sin is death" (Rom. 6:23), and the physical death of the body is linked by him to the rebellion of man against his creator's will; that is to say, death is not the will of God, but rather the direct result of the revolt against his will. Paul says further, "For as by a man came death, by a man has come also the resurrection of the dead. For as in Adam all die, so also in Christ shall all be made alive" (I Cor. 15:21-22); again, the physical death of man is linked with "Adam," that is, with man's corrupt condition.

We must distinguish between "death" as physical dying and "death" with its Christian aura of "new life beyond death." What God brings *out* of our physical death, the way in which he brings good out of it and brings "life and immortality to light," is not our concern at this moment. The physical death, the process

---

[6] There is to be noted the possibility of coming to *love* One Who Hurts. This is a perversion, but it is not too difficult to find in some "religious" experience.

and experience of dying, is in itself the outcome of evil and is so seen to be. Death is seen as *wrong,* as the final blow, the last helpless indignity; "the last enemy to be destroyed is death," says Paul—the last *enemy,* not friend. When Paul says that he longs to be with the Lord, he speaks of the Christian faith which sees past death and beyond the grave to the immortal life in Christ; but of the fact of death itself, he can only say that it is an enemy.

And so say all of us. On the physical level, facing the physical fact, the ultimate, inevitable fact of our lives, few of us are ready or willing to face the fact *as if it were good.* As believers we may earnestly and sincerely long for the time when we shall be with the Lord, in the communion of saints, beyond the touch of pain and death, reunited in the presence of God with those whom we have "loved and lost awhile"; but we wish it were all possible without going through the process of dying—that we might be "translated," that some sweet chariot would swing low and pluck us into eternal life without the dreaded intervention of death. As Christians we long for eternal life; but as men facing the fact of dying, we see it as no good thing. As Milton Mayer points out in his essay "On Death":

At any and every cost, we hang on—still we hang on for dear life. . . . Proof enough of the life instinct if (as

69

Goethe and Luther insist) the bargain is a bad one, and *we still cling to it.* . . . And still we are afraid to die. Give me my choice, to die tonight in an airplane crash or ten years from now in long, lonely pain, and I will try my cunning and say "Make it fifteen—make it twenty." [7]

It is a genuine and spontaneous cry of the heart in protest that Dylan Thomas expresses for us in his moving lines:

> Do not go gentle into that good
>   night;
> Old age should burn and rave at
>   close of day;
> Rage, rage against the dying of
>   the light.
>
> And you, my father, there on the
>   sad height,
> Curse, bless, me now with your
>   fierce tears, I pray.
> Do not go gentle into that good night.
> Rage, rage against the dying of the light. [8]

Some may talk of the "great adventure" and of how grand it is to die, but they are alive when they say it and

[7] *Great Ideas of Today* (Chicago: Encyclopaedia Britannica, 1965), pp. 135, 141.

[8] From *Collected Poems.* Copyright 1953 by Dylan Thomas, copyright 1957 by New Directions. Reprinted by permission of New Directions Publishing Corp., J. M. Dent and Sons, Ltd., and the literary executors of the Dylan Thomas estate.

in no imminent danger of having to prove their words. The bravery is usually bravado and, under all the talk of "greeting death as a friend," there is a blunt awareness that in cold fact we greet it as an enemy; only if we are in such pain or anguish as cannot be borne, does death seem a preferable alternative.

Sometimes in our days of strength and vigor we talk of death as a "blessing coming when life has benignly finished its course"; but we do not talk so when we are old, unless so crippled, lonely, or infirm that death seems the lesser of two evils; and even then it is resisted even by those who say they want it. At best, it is always and only the lesser of two evils, not good in itself. The old would agree with Maurice Chevalier who, when asked if he resented growing old, replied with his inimitable charm, "Not when you consider the alternative." It is the young, the healthy, the flourishing who string together brave words about death, for it seems far enough away to be spoken of without having to prove their words, yet even they know that beneath the surface of brave words, they are like children whistling for courage in the dark.

Rupert Brooke, who was himself to die so young, caught the sharp pathos in a sonnet's close:

"We are earth's best, that learnt her lesson here.
Life is our cry. We have kept the faith!" we said;

"We shall go down with unreluctant tread
Rose-crowned into the darkness! . . ." Proud we were,
And laughed, that had such brave true things to say.
And then you suddenly cried, and turned away.[9]

I must remind you again that I am talking of death
as the physical fact, not the believer's hope or certainty
of immortal life. The believer, no less than the non-
believer, has to face the physical fact, and he shies away
from it in much the same way. I believe most surely
in eternal life and I look forward to it with eagerness,
but I do not want to die, in the physical sense. For as
Teilhard de Chardin, talking also of physical death,
says:

In death, as in an ocean, all our slow or swift diminishments flow out and merge. Death is the sum and con-
summation of all our diminishments; it is *evil* itself—
purely physical evil, in so far as it results organically from
the material plurality in which we are immersed—but a
moral evil too, in so far as this disordered plurality, the
source of all strife and all corruption, is engendered in
society or in ourselves by the wrong use of our liberty.[10]

As Christians we know that God has conquered death,
that it has no holding power; but it is not part of the
Christian answer to pretend that death, physical death,

[9] "The Hill," from *Collected Poems* (New York: Dodd, Mead &
Co., 1961), p. 62.
[10] *The Divine Milieu,* p. 54.

the process of dying, is good or desirable in itself, or that it is anything but an enemy, the last enemy, which only God can overcome.

It is idle to speculate on what might have been the position of humanity if there had been no revolt against God, no "fall." Questions about population and over-crowding if there were no death are meaningless, for we have no idea what kind of world there would be if man had not rebelled. Anyone's guess is as good as the next man's. Our only experience is of a corrupt world and a corrupt humanity, and our great concern is God's action, redemptively, within this situation. Obviously, in this situation, death is a "necessity," but it is a neces-sity imposed by a situation which cannot be described as being in accordance with God's will. The Son of Man, faced with man's dying, prayed that he might be spared it. His prayer is every man's prayer.

Yet we have to face the fact that to many Christians death—physical death—seems to be not only God's in-tention but to come at God's precise and predetermined moment. They say that the time of death is an appointed one, fixed and ordained in God's immutable purpose; therefore they say, "When it's your time to go, it's your time to go," and "God will take you when it's your time" (and they do not see that, in this context, their use of the word "take" is a euphemism for "kill"). I firmly believe that God in his mercy will take me, in the sense of "receive" me when I go, but not that he will kill me off at some predetermined moment. Between some earnest Christians who talk of God's will and the Arabs with whom I worked in Algeria during World War II, who shrugged their shoulders in the face of death and disaster and said, "Kismet; it is written," I find too little difference. They are both fatalists, and I am not; for Christ is not.

This fatalistic view, which passes for faith among so many Christians, leads to a strange picture of life as a puppet show. If they are right and our time to go is appointed inexorably by him, we must picture God as gathering into an airplane a hundred people whose "time it is to die," all together in one prearranged crash. On the same theory one must presume that the hundreds of thousands who died in the split-second, split-atom ruin of Hiroshima were all predestined to die at that precise moment, and the atom bomb becomes the instrument by which the will of God was carried out. How absurd, to the point of blasphemy, can one get! Yet I can introduce you to many earnest and devout church members who sincerely accept the premise that leads to such a dreadful conclusion.

Sin, suffering, and death are not his will; he has not ordained them; he does not arrange them. As ugly stains spattered on his plan and purpose for us, they have come from without. "An enemy has done this."

5

THE ORIGIN OF SUFFERING

O that you had hearkened to my commandments!
Then your peace would have been like a river,
and your righteousness like the waves of the sea.

Isa. 48:18

Statement Six. All suffering is due to sin. And this statement is open, wide open, to disagreement. So let me make plain what I intend this statement to say and not to say. It says again, quite bluntly, that God is not the author of suffering and that therefore the author of suffering must be the revolt against God—sin. It says again that if suffering is good, then it is God's work; but if it is bad, then it cannot be his work. I have maintained that suffering is, in itself, evil and therefore cannot be his doing and must, therefore, be due to sin. If suffering is good, as some would say (sadism or masochism at work again?), then it must be in God, and suffering becomes part of the Godhead. As we say that God is love and that God is truth, so we must say that God is pain. But in fact, of course, suffering is part of the penalty brought on man by man, the result of man's fall and the work of evil. Suffering, pain, and death are to be abolished in God's good time, and the very fact that they are to *go,* and to go forever, means that they should never have been. They are not God's; they are not good.

But here we must be on our guard most carefully to make plain what this statement does *not* say, for a misunderstanding of man's responsibility for suffering can lead to some hideous mental cruelty. It does not say that we are necessarily directly responsible for all that we endure. I have known a church member to go to someone in suffering and say quite bluntly, "You must have done something terrible for God to punish you with this suffering." This is abominable, but it happens. In one of James Bridie's plays, one character describes another with these devastating words: "She was a good *Christian* woman, but hard and cruel." [1] In such a case as this, the description fits.

There are two big flaws in her brutal remark. The

[1] James Bridie, *Mary Read,* Act 1, Sc. 1.

first, of course, is that God does not send suffering; this
has been the constant theme through all I have said.
The second is that the principle of cause and effect is
not necessarily immediate as she assumed. We all protest against such an assumption, that each man's suffering is the result of his own sin, meted out in strict and
direct proportion to his sinfulness. This revolts us when
we see some sincere and lovely Christian, born in weak-
ness, living a gracious, pain-filled life, while some pagan
lives in health and strength; to go in such a case and
say "You are suffering for your sins" is not only un-
true, it is an infliction of further suffering.

Nor can we say to such a person, "God has chosen
you and given you an extra burden of suffering to bear
in the Christian spirit to his glory" (all too often said),
for I maintain that this accuses God of sadism. Nor can
we say, as is said with a seeming piety, that God gives
retarded children to special people so that they may
exhibit special grace. I know with humble admiration
that many such parents do, with God's help, show a
grace and patience that put the rest of us to shame; but
to suggest that God *creates* deliberately the retarded and
the crippled is to call him less than the God and Father
of our Lord Jesus Christ. As Jesus said:

What man of you, if his son asks him for a loaf, will give
him a stone? Or if he asks for a fish, will give him a

serpent? If you then, who are evil, know how to give good gifts to your children, how much more will your Father who is in heaven give good things to those who ask him! (Matt. 7:9-11.)

What merely human father would show his "love" by making his child deformed or retarded and say, "I am doing this to you so that others may be given a special opportunity for grace"? What merely human parent would show his "love" by inflicting suffering and say, "I am doing it for your own good, because I love you; and the more I love you, the more I hurt you"? Is God the Father less than a decent man? The minute we attribute the infliction of pain and death to God, we lose sight of the truth and all our thinking about him becomes distorted.

Further, there is something repellent to us in the idea of *undeserved* suffering. If it is true that man is responsible for sin, why should it be some good man, some fine Christian, who suffers so painfully when it is not his direct responsibility? Why should it be some little child, who may not be "innocent" because it is part of corrupt humanity but is certainly not responsible? Is this not bitterly unfair and cruel? The good Mr. Allworthy, Tom Jones' guardian, protests:

But to represent the Almighty as avenging the sins of the guilty on the innocent, was indecent, if not blasphemous, as it was to represent Him acting against the first principles of natural justice, and against the original notions of right and wrong, which He himself had implanted in our minds; by which we were to judge not only in all matters which were not revealed, but even of the truth of revelation itself.[2]

And heartily we agree, for this chimes in with all our sense of right and justice. How then must we say that man is responsible for sin and therefore for suffering?

We must distinguish between two main areas of suffering; they are not absolutely unrelated and may very often overlap, but they can be stated separately for the sake of clarity. The first is the kind of suffering which is due to our own sin and for which we are plainly responsible. If a man drinks heavily and gets cirrhosis of the liver, he is suffering for his own folly and self-indulgence; there is a direct, immediate, causal relationship between the two. If you like a lot of candy and neglect to brush your teeth, you can hardly wonder why you get toothaches; your greed and neglect have brought it on you. This is obvious, and most of us see very clearly in our own lives, and probably still more clearly in the lives of others, this direct and causal relationship between sin and *some* suffering.

However, we know the other cases where we can see

[2] Fielding, *Tom Jones,* Book 2, chap. 2.

no direct cause, no reason, no fairness, no chance at all to say, "Well, you asked for it and you got it." What are we to say? Like Mr. Allworthy we protest the idea that God avenges the sins of the guilty on the innocent; but as long as we cling to the idea that God is the author and sender of suffering, we shall be forced to that unhappy conclusion, and shall be tempted, under our seeming acceptance of "his will," to build up that bitterness and resentment against him of which I have written. As soon as we recognize that suffering is not sent from God, the difficulty disappears. We ask, "Is it not unfair and unjust that so often the good suffer most?" And we answer, "Yes it is; it *is* unfair and unjust, but that is a sign of the sinfulness of suffering, the evil of its origin." We ask, "Is it not unfair that the innocent should suffer for the guilty?" And we answer, "Yes it is. But then, we are dealing with evil and it works in evil ways. What else could we expect? It is unfair and unjust, because it is opposed to God's will, which is health and peace and joy."

The fact of suffering is unchanged. We still have to suffer and watch others suffer; but our attitude to it, to its origin and cause, is changed and, still more vital, our whole attitude toward God in the situation of suffering is changed. We no longer feel that we have to squeeze, somehow, life's bitterest blows into "his love"; we no longer feel that the hand of God has sent this upon us, either in punishment for our own sins or in avenging the sins of our forebears on their descendents—or, for that matter, as an "opportunity for grace." We can now turn to him for help, comfort, strength, power to overcome, knowing that he has not sent the grief and that he is urgent to help us overcome it. No longer are we in the strange position of asking him to abolish and overcome what he has deliberately sent. We know that we are part of mankind, bound in one bundle of life. We share a common humanity, corrupted and sinful. We share in the blessings of our common humanity, in the fruits of the labors of others; we also share in the disease of our common humanity, suffering, sometimes out of all proportion, unjustly, unfairly, because we are part of this broken mirror, this damaged image of God. And we know that if it is unfair, it is so not because God is unfair but because it is evil. When cancer strikes, it is evil striking; remember that Paul calls his thorn in the flesh a messenger of Satan, not a messenger of God. When a child is killed on the streets, it is evil at work. When an earthquake destroys lives, it is evil shaking the world. When thousands die in the searing blast of a bomb, it is evil working its destruction. When death comes quietly and unexpectedly, leaving a break in a family that no one else can fill, it is an evil thing— part of man's deep legacy of sin and rebellion, in which we are all heirs, because we are men; and because we are sinful, often bitterly unfair and unjust. But what else would we expect of sin?

You may notice that I have throughout tacitly excluded the possible operation of a "third force"—call it chance, luck, or accident as you will. We talk frequently and easily of chance, luck, and accident as if they did exist, as if they constituted such a third force not attributable to God's will or man's action. We use the idea in both major and minor matters. Writing in the preface to his major *Interpretation of Dreams* Freud says that it contains "the most valuable of all discoveries it has been my good fortune to make. Insight such as this falls to one's lot but once in a lifetime." [3] But we must ask if he uses "fortune" and "lot" seriously, as expressing his view of how he came to a major psychological discovery, or whether he uses the words merely as convenient tokens. Surely it is the latter; he does not know exactly how this discovery came about, nor is he concerned at the moment with the causality, so he uses fortune and lot (as we all do) to avoid having to dig into the question, irrelevant at the moment, of how this came to him.

It is equally useful in minor matters; for example, we are one day in a great hurry, late for an appointment, and just as we reach our destination, a car pulls out and leaves us with an unhoped-for parking space. Later we

[3] Preface to third English edition, p. 135.

tell someone, "I was so lucky—I got a parking space right at the door." "Lucky"; "fortunate." Do we mean it seriously? Do we mean that there is a third force which is "accident"—in the strict sense of "it just happens"? To say in such circumstances, as earlier and more pious generations might, "God provided for me" rightly seems to us unbearably smug and complacent (though, if the occasion is urgent enough, we moderns too may feel that there is some beneficent deity who kindly causes a car to move so that we may find room to park. We may even say piously "Thank God," little thinking that for all we know the man who moved out may have left because he had heard news of some disaster at his home which will wreck his peace of mind and break his heart. It is always good to thank God, but not if in so doing we imply that God is bouncing others around in order to accommodate us). In actual fact the cause of the other car moving is so completely unknown to us (and in general so irrelevant to us) that we do better to talk of "luck" and "chance," provided we do not take the words literally, realizing that these words are just coins we use on all occasions when the causation is too hidden for us to see, or too remote from our interest. Most of us would agree with Tolstoy that chance "does not denote any really existing thing" but only "a certain stage of understanding of phenomena." To take seriously the idea that there are events that

83

just happen, independent of God's will or man's action, would be to live in a world of frightening uncertainty. Though we may talk of "fortune" we believe that everything has a cause, however obscure to us, and that it happens within God's knowledge. Further, we believe that everything that "happens" is under God's ultimate control; but this is to anticipate. It is enough for the moment to repeat that whatever is hurtful is not the will of God.

As most of us think most easily in terms of particular examples, let us refer again to some of the cases—general but all too real—with which this book opened. A car skids and overturns; we can think of many possible causes—human error on the part of the driver; a fault, through carelessness or miscalculation, in the structure or contour of the road; the failure of a bearing or a tire, due to bad workmanship or bad maintenance; a careless mechanic, unaware or unheeding of his responsibility for the safety of others; or any of a dozen other causes. But does God, the perfect, the holy, the loving, employ error, carelessness, bad workmanship as the means of doing his will?

The boy is killed by the drunken driver. Can drunkenness be God's chosen and deliberate way of working— the degradation of the body to a drug and the stupefying of the mind and higher faculties? Is this not sin and only sin? Cancer strikes. It may, according to increasing medical evidence, be a direct result of excessive smoking (and are we then driven to condemn smoking on Christian grounds if it has such a result?), or it may be in no conceivable way directly connected with the victim, but rather part of the whole diseased state of corrupt humanity. In both cases, whether direct or indirect, it is contrary to God's will and is the result of sin. So with every instance, and so with the seemingly senseless and brutal disasters of nature; we realize that they *are* senseless and brutal, because they are violations of God's will in a corrupt world.

Why then, we cry, does God permit it? Obviously he does, but why? If he is wholly good and utterly loving and completely just, why does he allow it? It is the old cry of the human heart in its anguish, and we must give an answer. Some, as we have seen, try to answer by saying that he does it all himself and that someday we shall see why and find that it was really all for the best. I for one cannot so easily deny the fact of evil and the deep awareness that suffering is the work of sin, not of God.

We cry to him to "stop it," but really that means that we cry to him to stop *us*—to remove our freedom, to deprive us of the liberty to choose and decide and act. As long as we are free and corrupt, we are free to sin, to hurt others and be hurt by them; free to take part in the good and bad of our common humanity; *free*.

On the basis of our frantic cry to God to "stop it," there is no answer that does not involve taking away from us the very thing that makes us men, not animals —mind, reason, will. We are men, and given the choice between the abolition of all sin and suffering at the cost of losing our freedom, or on the other hand keeping our freedom, our essential humanity, even if it involves suffering, would anyone really ask to have his freedom taken away?

God gave man freedom; we have gloried in it; we (all men) have abused it; we suffer for that abuse (not just our own but for all mankind's sin in all the centuries). How could it be changed, by any arbitrary word from God, as if by a magician's wand, without depriving us of the freedom which has opened the way to sin and suffering? In any case the choice is not the creature's but the Creator's; not ours but his; and he has chosen; and he has chosen to leave us free.

We are free to sin. We are men.

6

THE PREDICAMENT OF MAN

"I can will what is right, but I cannot do it." Rom. 7:18

We are free to sin. Yes, but is that all, as many earnest Christians would assert? Has our will become so corrupted that we are now free only to sin, and not free at all to do good? Have we any power left to us to want and prefer and will the good?

Statement Seven. Man's free will is impaired through his sin, but is not destroyed. Here again we are in an area of vitally important disagreement. How far is man's will impaired? Can he will any good at all, or is the power to will good and to choose obedience utterly lost to him? How hopeless is his predicament?

The Westminster Confession of Faith, one of the most influential and formative documents since the Reformation, is unambiguous:

By this sin they fell from their original righteousness and communion with God, and so became dead in sin, and wholly defiled in all the faculties and parts of soul and body.

They being the root of all mankind, the guilt of this sin was imputed, and the same death in sin and corrupted nature conveyed to all their posterity, descending from them by ordinary generation.

From this original corruption, whereby we are utterly indisposed, disabled, and made opposite to all good, and wholly inclined to all evil, do proceed all actual transgressions.[1]

"Utterly indisposed, disabled, and made opposite to all good." Nothing could be plainer. The truth that is in it needs to be stated and restated; for while some existentialists have reached a level of despair of man's condition and hopelessness about his future (a despair far darker even than the Confession's), much of the world is still tinged with a rosy humanism, still impossibly believing that man can pull himself out of the mud by his own shoestrings, in spite of all the evidence of crime and war, in spite of the inner evidence of man's

[1] Westminster Confession of Faith, chap. 6, sections II, III, IV.

self-defeating, self-destroying energy of which sin and war are the outward manifestations. Nor is this only a modern heresy, for Pelagius in the fifth century advocated much the same optimistic humanism in his own day and won (as such a cheerful doctrine is apt to do) considerable support. Pelagianism has always been branded as heresy by the church and branded as folly by those, inside or outside the church, who are willing to look beneath the surface of technical achievement and see the unhappy fact of man's predicament—a predicament made more acute by the technical powers which urgently demand an adequate moral power in control. Each new disaster shakes the fond hope that man has the power to save himself; but all too quickly, as the lull between conflicts lures men back into self-confidence, humanism in one form or another increases, and the hope grows again that this time, surely this time, man will go on to Utopia. If nothing else, the history of our time might drive us back to the doctrine of the corruption of man's nature.

But a healthy eagerness to avoid the danger of humanism must not draw us into the opposite extreme. The answer to a wild optimism is not an equally wild pessimism. Principal Denney wrote:

Our whole nature is involved in sin, but not indistinguishably and irretrievably involved, and we disown the sin and protest against it even when we feel ourselves most hopelessly its slaves. On this the need and the possibility of redemption depend. There may be a doctrine of human depravity, not only seriously expressing serious facts, but so exaggerated and uncompromising as to exclude the very possibility of redemption. . . . We must hold such a doctrine of sin as makes it evident that we cannot save ourselves, but not such a doctrine as implies that not even God can save us.[2]

Corrupt man is, indeed, but is he so corrupt that he can neither desire nor do any good of his own volition? Can he not take even the first step toward right; or, as a leg that has "gone to sleep" feels the impulse to move but cannot, can he at least want to turn to God? Is it a denial of man's corruption to claim that he still has the ability at least to *want* even if he has no power to *do?* If the doctrine of man's utter helplessness is carried to the limit, we are brought to the full, rigid doctrine of election and predestination—that, as man is utterly lost, only God can rouse the human heart even to want good, still more to respond to it; and if this is the case, if man is wholly and completely dependent on God's action, then obviously it is God who must choose to arouse a particular man and make him even willing to want new life as a first step to receiving it. And from there you

[2] James Denney, *The Christian Doctrine of Reconciliation* (London: Hodder & Stoughton, 1917), p. 199.

are carried by logic to the corollary that if it is wholly dependent on God's choice, then he must also choose *not* to rouse others and bring them to new life, but rather to send them to hell and damnation. As the Westminster Confession of Faith puts it:

By the decree of God, for the manifestation of his glory, some men and angels are predestinated unto everlasting life, and others fore-ordained to everlasting death.

The rest of mankind, God was pleased, according to the unsearchable counsel of his own will, whereby he extendeth or withholdeth mercy as he pleaseth, for the glory of his sovereign power over his creatures, to pass by, and to ordain them to dishonour and wrath for their sin, to the praise of his glorious justice.[3]

And somewhere in the background old Dr. Johnson snorts, "Sir, we are free and we know it and that is an end of it." As the British Light Brigade charged its glorious and deathly charge against the guns at Balaclava, a French general, watching the futile splendor, said with Gallic realism, "It is magnificent, but it is not war." So perhaps some, seeing the Confession's charge against the guns of human pride, may be inclined to sigh, "It is magnificent, but it is not Christianity."

Now let there be a warning about logic and love,

[3] Chap. 3, sections III, VII.

which, as I mentioned in the first chapter, do not always go along together. Or rather, there are two kinds of logic—the logic of reason and the logic of love. The logic of reason needs little explanation; it is familiar to all of us; it leads us sometimes to great conclusions, and sometimes to damnable conclusions. It is a good servant but a dangerous master. The logic of love achieves things that are "impossible" to reason. I have seen it, time and time again, in action. I have seen situations where every argument of logic foretold a certain conclusion, until love came in and brushed "reason" aside and did "unreasonable" things and broke rules and barriers and achieved impossible results. If you have no cause in your own life to look back and see what love has done that reason said could not be done, then I pity you. I bear witness to you, that love finds ways where there are none; and I solemnly warn you that, if you ignore this, you can be logical to the limit and still be utterly wrong. This should come as no surprise, for we know that the final power in the world is not reason but love; so that if we would come anywhere near to understanding the final power in the universe, we must beware of moving simply by the logic of reason without the logic of love to correct; for as love is so often "unreasonable," reason is so often unloving.

This is the danger of all closely formulated and detailed creeds; reason guides their construction, as is understandable, and is a fallible guide. God is not to be comprehended by human reason. In the first chapter of Isaiah there is a scene of a trial—the epitome of reason and logic. Evidence is brought and examined and weighed—evidence of the guilt of Israel. Reason is satisfied that Israel is guilty and to be punished; reason and justice demand it. Then, just as logic and reason have reached their climax, "Come and let us bring our reasoning to a close, says the Lord, though your sins be as scarlet they shall be white as snow" (Isa. 1:18).[4] Utterly unexpected, quite unreasonable, wholly illogical! But again love with its own logic has broken through the rigid legalism of reason. And with which would you rather have to deal? So, in all our thinking and argument and reasoning, let this be always in our minds, that we may have all the knowledge and understanding and reason in the world, but if we do not have an understanding of love's strange and wonderful ways, we shall misunderstand it all. This is the "more excellent way" that Paul commends to us.

Now take that passage of Isaiah one verse farther: "If only you are willing to obey." What does this mean? Either it means that man has some power, at least to be willing, or else it is an empty phrase. If man is utterly impotent, how can he be called on to be

[4] *Expositor's Bible,* tr. by Sir George Adam Smith (Hodder & Stoughton), p. 13.

willing to obey? This is of vital importance as we think of the ministry of our Lord, who went about calling on men to listen, to follow, to obey, to have faith; do we imagine that he called on them to do what he knew to be impossible? Or does it mean that he called on that lingering spark of man's God-given freedom and then fanned it, as only he could, into a fire of new life and liberty through faith in him?

For God asks, "Who will go for us?" God waits for the answer. He does not compel. Isaiah's decision to go must be free. Freedom of decision is the second condition of prophetic existence. A prophet must decide whether or not he will dedicate himself to the task. With respect to our fate and vocation we are free; with respect to our relation to God we are powerless. The majesty of God is evident in either case.[5]

If man is so lost that he can no more respond and is dependent entirely on some direct action of God to enable him to answer, then the ministry of Jesus is reduced to a piece of playacting. He appealed to men, he called, he demanded. "He who has ears, let him hear"; "follow me"; "have faith"—these are real calls to some lingering ability in man to respond. As we read the Gospels we do not get the impression that Jesus spoke to men whom he regarded as "utterly indisposed, dis-

[5] Tillich, *The Shaking of the Foundations,* p. 91.

abled, and made opposite to all good," but that he spoke to the faint flicker of man's original goodness, and the reality and poignancy of his appeal depend on that condition. It approaches a charge of questionable sincerity to maintain that he appealed to men who were quite unable to respond to his appeal; that he called to follow him men who were utterly unable to obey; that all his pleading with the human heart was really a mockery because he knew that the issues had long ago been decided; that none could hear him and live except by a deliberate choice of God to let that man hear and live; and that those who never responded were left unable to respond by a deliberate choice of God, who chose to let them reject and die. This is a puppet show. This is not the Gospel.

The old cry will rise that to hold that man has some trace of freedom is to challenge the sovereignty and grace of God; that to suggest that man could choose anything good takes away from the glory of God. This, of course, is nonsense. All goodness is from God; the goodness mankind had in his origin was given by God; any goodness man has left in him comes from God. There is no goodness except from God. All that is good is his, and all that is his is good. So the goodness that lingers still in man is the lingering gift of God, and when a man uses that spark of goodness, the praise and glory are God's not man's. What little goodness man

95

does have has been given; but he does have it. He still has the power to reject or accept, however twisted his nature. He still has the responsibility of decision. He has them, not to his own credit or by his own power but because God has given them to him.

> Not in entire forgetfulness,
> And not in utter nakedness,
> But trailing clouds of glory do we come
> From God who is our home.[6]

If God's sovereignty is challenged by the fraction of freedom left to man and by his faint, lingering ability to recognize and choose good, then how much more the sovereignty of God must have been challenged when, before the fall, man was wholly good and free! We must be clear that goodness in the creature is not a rival to the power and omnipotence of God, for the goodness is derivative, given by the power of the God who has willed that man shall be free. If man's original full goodness was no challenge, neither is man's remaining spark of goodness, nor is man's ultimate goodness in the new heaven and earth; for all goodness comes from God.

And of God's gift, a little—so little, yet a little—remains.

[6] Wordsworth, "Ode: Intimations of Immortality."

7

THE APPROACH OF GOD

"I came that they may have life." John 10:10

Statement Eight. All men are elect and called. In God's original purpose, men, all men, were to be for fellowship and service with him and for him. Man was created, elect, chosen by God for his praise and glory. Man was created for freedom not bondage, for good not wrong, for glory not shame. All mankind, in origin, is elect and all mankind is called by God.

Now man is a fallen creature, a corrupted being who, though he has a lingering spark of God's gift left in him, is unable to save himself or pull himself out of the mud. Man's will is enfeebled but is not destroyed. He must be lifted out of the mud by outside help, for he is too weak to help himself; he needs to be saved and cannot save himself. But on the determinist, predestinarian premise, man is so utterly disabled that he can do *nothing,* and it all comes to God's choice—will he save him or will he not? Will he put this man in the "elect" category or the "nonelect"? Will God make him a sheep or a goat? Man is seen as mere clay in the potter's hand, and some will be chosen and shaped, others will be rejected and thrown away. It is all, wholly and utterly, up to a divine choice, and we are asked to praise God not only for saving some (among whom, for all our protestations, we tacitly assume ourselves to be) but also for damning others. This, I repeat, is not the Gospel. No wonder that those who write about predestination warn against talking and thinking about it too much.

So, for curious and carnal persons, lacking the Spirit of Christ, to have continually before their eyes the sentence of God's pre-destination, is a most dangerous downfal, whereby the devil doth thrust them either into desperation, or into wretchlessness of most unclean living, no less perilous than desperation.[1]

This is unfair! "Don't let the damned know they're damned in case they act as men who have nothing

[1] The Articles of Religion of the Church of England, Article 17.

98

more to lose and are a damned nuisance to us who are elect." There is something far wrong with a fundamental point of Christian belief if it has to be hushed up and not discussed.

I believe that the whole Gospel message, which is the astounding logic of love, lights up the scene and shows the absurdity and the near sacrilege of the logic of reason with its picture of an arbitrary decision to "save this one and to hell with that." So I repeat, not just of the past in the first creation but of here and now: all men are elect and called. As the 1960 creed of the United Church of Christ says: "He seeks in holy love to save all people from aimlessness and sin."

This is not universalism, claiming that somehow or other all *will* be saved, willy-nilly.[2] It is not a statement of accomplished fact, but a statement of purpose— God's purpose as we see it in Christ. All men are elect in the sense that God loves and wants and hopes for the salvation of all. The real distinction is not between the elect and the nonelect; it is between those who in

[2] Universalism may, in fact, be more easily tied to a strongly predestinarian position; for if "those to be saved will be saved," it may be, for all that we know, that God has decreed that all *are* to be saved and are all "elect." Universalism is next to impossible on the argument of human freedom, for it holds that, to the very end, man can reject him. I should like nothing better than to be able to believe that all will be saved in the end, even the worst; but I know too much of the human heart, and of my own heart, and I know that even on the precipice of hell man can shake his fist at God and refuse his offered grace.

Christ accept their election and those who, though equally elect in his purpose, refuse to accept it. Even the great picture of the judgment in Matthew 25:31 ff. bases the judgment not on an eternal decree of predestination to life for some and to damnation for others, but on man's response to God's appeal—the opportunity for love and service given equally to all, and the possibility of responding which is real for all. "The kingdom that has been prepared" has been prepared for all, and God longs to gather them all, but only some are willing. "The readiness is all."

We read how Jesus wept over the old and arrogant city of Jerusalem and spoke the city's epitaph: "O Jerusalem, Jerusalem, killing the prophets and stoning those who are sent to you! How often would I have gathered your children together as a hen gathers her brood under her wings, and you would not!" Here is plainly stated man's freedom and responsibility, for implicit in the words is the real hope and possibility that man could and would accept, but refused. "You would not." Here too is what we may call the "helplessness" of God in the face of human intransigence; he cannot, he will not force obedience; it must come in some way from the man himself, from his free choice. This is no puppet show; this is God in his relationship to man.

Most important for our present statement, here is expressed in plain and moving words what we see through the whole of his life and teaching—the yearning of God for his children, for all men; his wish to gather them all together as a hen her brood of chickens. He does not cry out, "You that are elect in my Father's purpose will be gathered together, and you who are non-elect in his purpose will be damned to his great glory and praise." The words in the mouth of Christ are unimaginable. So let this lead us here to a major statement.

Statement Nine. God is made known in Christ. This must underlie and cohere with everything we say about God's will. Turn to John 14:8. Philip had appealed to him—such a human and understandable appeal—"Lord, show us the Father, and we shall be satisfied." Just to see God, understand him, recognize his hand, perceive his purpose—a most human cry! The answer is given to him and to us, the answer which is the touchstone by which the truth or falsity of every statement about God's will must be tested. Jesus said to him, "He who has seen me has seen the Father." And there you have it, clear, unequivocal. It is, of course, the most astounding claim ever made, and of the man who made it you must say one of two things; either he is right or he is crazy. Either he is God incarnate, or he is, if sincere, a megalomaniac; or if insincere, the biggest charlatan that ever lived. As Christian people we believe with all our hearts that God was in Christ, that Jesus was God incarnate; and this is the foundation on which we build.

That being so, look at the implications. To see Jesus is to see God—no less; so that what is in Christ is in God, and what is in God is in Christ. Christ is God revealed to us. Therefore it follows that we may not say anything of God which we cannot equally happily say of Christ; nor say anything of Christ which we are not prepared to say of God. Yet how many good church people have two very dissimilar pictures in mind; they have an Old Testament God and a New Testament Christ; they have an angry God and a loving Jesus; they have a God who ordains men to damnation for his glory and a Savior who seeks to gather them all together as a hen her brood of chickens under her wings. God has a split personality for many Christians who cannot dare to believe, really believe, what Jesus tells them here, that to see him is to see God. Most of our strange distortions come from this point of confusion. Consider three typical distortions.

1. The first is that we often attribute to God actions we should not dream of attributing to Christ, and many of our formal, logical, creedal statements about God and his ways can hardly be transferred without a shock to the Lord Jesus Christ. For example,

I do not read in the Gospels that Jesus said to a sick man who asked for healing, "Suffering is good and is sent by God, and as I am here to do my Father's will,

I cannot possibly interfere. So, my dear friend, you must suffer, for it is God's will." The absurdity of putting such words into the mouth of Jesus shocks us; but these are the very words which so many attribute to God.

I do not read in the Gospels that Jesus said to a father who, in faith and love, brought his retarded child for healing, "God in his great wisdom sends exceptional children to special parents so that they may show special grace, so I cannot deprive you of this great privilege." We cannot imagine him saying it, therefore we must not imagine that God says it.

I do not read in the Gospels that Jesus told Jairus, the ruler of the synagogue, "I am sorry for you that your daughter is dying, but if it is her time to die, it is her time to die, and it is all predetermined by my Father." Again, the idea of such words from him dismays us; but "I and the Father are one," and if we can say it about God the Father, we must be able to say it about God the Son. And if we cannot bring ourselves to say it about Jesus, we cannot say it about God.

I do not read in the Gospels that Jesus told the widow of Nain, as she carried her only son out to be buried, "This anguish is sent to you from God for your own ultimate good; it is from him who ordains whatever comes to pass, so I can do nothing about it. And in addition God marks his favored children with extra burdens of suffering to be borne to his glory; so go, woman, and bury your son."

I have often wondered why, if suffering is not evil, our Lord spent so much of his time and energy in fighting it; why he poured out his strength, so that "power went forth from him" to heal, and to heal them all. Wherever he went, the sick came or were brought to him and never once did he refuse to set them free. Why, why, why, if suffering is God's messenger? Unsparingly he gave himself in a ministry of healing, giving sight to the blind, hearing to the deaf, mobility to the crippled, release to the epileptic, sanity to the disturbed. For all its unscientific sound the biblical view of "devils" being responsible for illness comes right to the spiritual truth, that the suffering and sorrow and disturbance of body and mind are the work of evil, not of good; and so it was that Jesus spoke of them and dealt with them. And if it is true that "troubles are sent by God to try us," how can they be at the same time the work of "devils," of evil?

It is very strange how people can contradict themselves and be blithely unaware of it. A few may be as cold-bloodedly "Christian" as Mr. Thwackum in *Tom Jones,* for whom "charity seemed to be opposing the will of the Almighty, which had marked some particular persons for destruction," [3] but most of those who

---

[3] Fielding, Book 3, chap. 8.

say that "God sends us suffering" will go to all lengths to thwart that will, both for themselves and for others. They will seek healing and help from doctors and surgeons; they will support charities and hospitals; they will pray fervently to God to take away what they believe he has sent. In fact, as I have pointed out before, we may with the "top of our minds" accept a rigid doctrine that God "ordains whatever comes to pass," but the depth of the heart, the real life of man, lives by another rule.

2. A second distortion, resulting from the failure to remember that Christ is God revealed to us, is that we make God seem to "use" men as tools, mere instruments, in a way which we could not attribute to Jesus and, in fact, in a way which we would condemn in mere men. Men are souls not things, not to be "used" for purposes, even good purposes. As soon as we think of "using" people, manipulating them, even for seemingly good ends, we are in moral danger. This dialogue occurs in *The Deputy:*

CARDINAL: How could the Germans have forgotten the mission God assigned to them as the fulcrum of the West?

GERSTEIN (*softly*)*:* Your Eminence, that could not be. God would not be God if He made use of a Hitler . . .

105

CARDINAL: Oh yes, oh yes, most certainly, my friend! Was not even Cain, who killed his brother, the instrument of God?

Cain had his mission in the world, as Noah did. What can we know of the terrible detours of the Lord! [4]

Hochhuth puts into the mouth of his Cardinal that doctrine of preordination which is not only distinctive of churches with a strong Calvinist tradition but is to be found, as we have seen, in the Thirty-nine Articles of Religion of the Episcopal Church, and is not foreign to much Roman Catholic thought. And here again the false dichotomy between God and Christ leads men into wild conclusions in which God is conceived of as using men, almost ruthlessly, for his purposes. This same determinist trend appears when, later in the same act, Hochhuth gives Father Riccardo this:

RICCARDO: Could Judas have refused to play his role? He *knew* (*with an intense fear of his own conclusions*) he would be damned for all eternity. His sacrifice was greater than the Lord's. [5]

I have even known Judas be referred to as "that saint," because he had done God's will for him and had been

---

[4] Hochhuth, Act 3, Sc. 2, p. 148.
[5] *Ibid.*, p. 163.

the necessary instrument of God to bring Jesus to the cross. This in all seriousness! This, too, from someone who had read the pleading of our Lord by word and action, the foot washing, the bread dipped and given, the appeal of all love to Judas by every means possible to save him, *short of forcing him against his will.* Again I insist that God does not "use" men in this way; that the Gospel is not a puppet show in which motions are gone through, with the results already settled immutably, so that the appeal of Christ is not really an appeal at all, and the choice of Judas is not really a choice, because God has decided and chosen what Judas must and shall do. This makes a travesty out of the whole glorious appeal of our Lord to mankind.

Beware of talking of the "drama" of the Gospels; it is a dangerous metaphor if it leads you to think that the parts are all written and given to the players to go through the words and motions with no "ad-libbing" even possible! If Judas cannot help betraying his Lord, because God has so ordained it, Judas must be absolved of blame; and who can transfer that idea to Christ, without a feeling of blasphemy, and say that it was the will of Jesus that Judas should betray him, so that even as Jesus washed Judas' feet and appealed to his soul, Jesus had deliberately ordained that Judas should refuse! This is to accuse the Lord of insincerity and playacting, of treating men as mere puppets and tools, and it is blasphemous; and if, as is obvious, you cannot say it, dare not say it, about Jesus, you dare not say it about God, for "I and the Father are one."

3. It is out of our forgetfulness of this fact, that Christ and the Father are one, that the third distortion arises when we talk much of the "mystery" of God's ways, of his "inscrutable" will, of the impossibility of man's understanding his purposes and plans. That there is truth in it is plain, for the finite can never grasp the infinite, nor the creature fully comprehend the Creator. This much is plain, that we see at best in a dim mirror, and know at best only in part. But we *do* see, and we *do* know, even if it is only fractionally. Jesus said, "If you have seen me, you have seen the Father," and we have seen him, and therefore we have seen God. It is not all dark and mysterious; it is not all inscrutable and unknowable; we do not go through life with the meaning and purpose hidden from us. Jesus Christ came to show us God, to reveal God, to make known his nature and way; and if we are then still in the dark in the midst of life's problems, and if when sorrow comes we can only cry that his will is inscrutable, then Christ has failed in his declared purpose of making God known to us.

As a Christian I must say "I *do* understand God's will. I *do* see his purpose. I *do* know what his will is for me and mankind and the world, for Christ has declared it in his life and death and resurrection. Life is not all muddle and mystery; God is not unknowable and inscrutable. I *know,* even though only in part." Usually we take the latter part of Paul's thirteenth chapter of his first letter to Corinth as stressing the littleness of man's knowledge, but we should also take it as an affirmation of the great fact that in Christ we do know, even though only a little; that we do understand, even though most imperfectly. Christ has shown us God; we are no longer in the dark. We do not have to talk, like Hochhuth's Cardinal, of the "terrible detours of the Lord."

As we face life's problems of suffering and death, it is not enough for a Christian to cry, "God's will is beyond my understanding; it is a mystery. I must simply suffer and accept and hope some day to know why." For a pagan, yes; for a Christian, no. God was in Christ; Christ has revealed the Father. "If you have seen me you have seen the Father," he says; and we in glad response cry the joyful cry of Christians of all ages, "We have seen the Lord!" And because we have seen the Lord, we have seen God.

"I *know* whom I have believed."

8

THE CROSS OF CHRIST

"He had compassion." MATT. 9:36

We know whom we have believed; we know God through Jesus the Christ; we know that Jesus came into the world for a purpose, and that that purpose is our intimate concern. This purpose forms our next statement.

Statement Ten. Christ came into the world to save all men. Some time ago I read in a religious periodical an article which opened with these words: "Our Lord came into the world for the explicit purpose of dying for the sins of mankind." He did not. He came into the world for the explicit purpose of saving us from our corrupt state and of restoring us to fellowship with God, and, if a cross were the only way to do it, prepared to die for us. He himself prayed in Gethsemane that there might be a way to do it without the cross, but when there was no other way, he took the way of the cross.

So we find ourselves again in the realm of a determinism which would make the whole tragedy of man's refusal and the brutal horror of the cross part of the deliberate purpose of God; to many people, God is an angry God to be satisfied, and only to be satisfied by blood and pain. Aeschylus' Prometheus (who was a kind of benefactor and self-appointed savior of man) cries out:

> Mercy I had for man; and therefore I
> Must meet no mercy, but hang crucified
> In witness of God's cruelty and pride.[1]

Some Christians' picture of God is not so very far removed from the ancient pagan Greek. "He had to die because only death and blood and agony could satisfy the righteousness of God." Now if this is true, if only a cross could satisfy, was not the life of appeal and challenge a travesty? Why are men called to come to God if there is no way by which they can come except

[1] *Prometheus Bound,* p. 31, lines 241-43.

through blood and pain? This is God, not Moloch. God is not sadistic, inflicting pain on his children, insisting on suffering for satisfaction; God is not masochistic, inflicting pain on himself in the person of his Son, in order to satisfy himself. This is our human perversion transferred to God.

Christ Jesus came to save and, if need be, to die in order to save, but not to die for the sake of dying if there were no need. Douglas Webster, an admirer of P. T. Forsyth, writes:

God is not satisfied by pain or death as such but only by holiness. Thus, as Forsyth insists—and this is a most urgently needed corrective—the atoning thing is not the suffering but the holiness and obedience of the divine Son. God did not require pain or suffering or death as the means of atonement. He did require holy obedience. And the human situation being what it was, that holy obedience was bound to lead to pain and suffering and death. It did. But the salvation he procured was due to the holiness he offered to God on our behalf and not to any virtue in suffering undeserved pain. Holiness produces its own pain in a sinful world.[2]

Much traditional thinking of his death as a "propitiation" verges on the pagan; so too the idea behind the word "satisfaction." The picture of an offended God

[2] Douglas Webster, *In Debt to Christ* (Philadelphia: Fortress Press, 1964), chapter 2.

to be propitiated, satisfied, placated by sacrifice, by blood and death and nothing less, is one which the best of the Old Testament rejects. The psalmist says:

> For thou hast no delight in sacrifice;
>   were I to give a burnt offering,
>   thou wouldst not be pleased.
> The sacrifice acceptable to God is a broken spirit;
>   a broken and contrite heart, O
>   God, thou wilt not despise. (Ps. 51 :16-17.)

And Isaiah, proclaiming the word from the Lord:

> I have had enough of burnt offerings of rams
>   and the fat of fed beasts;
> I do not delight in the blood of bulls,
>   or of lambs, or of he-goats. (Isa. 1 :11.)

And Micah:

> Will the Lord be pleased with thousands of rams,
>   with ten thousands of rivers of oil?
> Shall I give my first-born for my transgression,
>   the fruit of my body for the sin of my soul?
> He has showed you, O man, what is good;
>   and what does the Lord require of you
> but to do justice, and to love kindness,
>   and to walk humbly with your God?
>   (Mic. 6 :7-8.)

Of his approaching death (which he saw to be inevitable, not because God wanted it but because a corrupt world could not tolerate the challenge of God's holiness) Jesus said that he gave his life as a "ransom" for many. Now when the victim of a kidnapping is held for ransom, and a ransom is paid so that he may be set free, the ransom is paid by whom, to whom? By the father of the kidnapped child to himself through his agent? Nonsense. By the father, through his agent, to the kidnapper, to the villain of the piece. The ransom that Christ paid is the price that evil demands, that sin inflicts. It is not paid as a propitiation to God to placate or satisfy him, but as a ransom to evil so that the victims may be set free. The metaphor must not be carried too far or taken too literally; it does not suggest that there was any agreement or bargain with evil; he did not mean that, for compromise with evil was out of the question. Similes and metaphors are at best illustrations and should not be pressed too far; however, this metaphor of "ransom" is his own and must be taken seriously.

If we want to think of his death as a sacrifice, we must think of it not as a sacrifice offered to God in order to satisfy or propitiate but as a sacrifice made and offered in the absolute service of God; not as demanded by God for satisfaction but as demanded by the desperate situation; and being freely and utterly made, therefore holy, and in that sense "pleasing" to God. If I may risk an analogy—when a man, in the ultimate service of his country, gives his life, we rightly talk of him as having made "the final sacrifice." This sacrifice is, in one sense, demanded of him by his country, but it is not demanded as "pleasing" or "satisfying"; rather it is the demand of love and duty, the demand that is not imposed from without but arises from within, from love and loyalty. There is nothing legalistic about it. His sacrifice is demanded as the only adequate response to a desperate situation, and the sacrifice is never thought of as being made *to* his country, but rather and only as made *for* his country. In some such way, I believe, Christ's sacrifice was made *for* the Father—in his absolute and ultimate service—not *to* the Father.

This is the heart of the matter. Christ came to save, and in so doing came into a world riddled with sin. The world had the clear and real choice of accepting or rejecting him; but such a world could not bear the perfection of Christ; sin cannot tolerate holiness, for holiness is an unbearable rebuke. In a world of sin goodness must suffer, not because it is God's will that it suffer, not because God requires suffering for satisfaction, but because a sinful world will resent goodness, make it suffer, even kill it. The infliction of suffering and death comes from the sin, not from God. God did not order the cross; he ordered holy obedience, and the world

115

put him on the cross because he was holy and obedient. Christ submitted himself to a human body and to earthly powers; and because the world is corrupt and man is sinful, they took him and nailed his body to a cross; *they* did it, not God. *They* required it, not the Father.

It is another matter of speculation to ask, "What if all men instead of just a few had repented and responded to him; or even if a majority of men had accepted him as Lord? Would the cross still have been a necessity?" If there had been no man wanting to crucify him, or if the majority had supported him, would he still have had to be crucified in order to "satisfy" God? Is the cross necessary in a primary sense or a secondary sense —absolutely necessary because God demanded it, or necessary because man's sin demanded it?

Dr. Weatherhead writes:

I believe, as we have said before, that the Cross was not the intention of God for Jesus. God's intention was that Jesus should be followed, not crucified. But when evil men thrust the Cross upon him, he accepted God's will in those circumstances and so reacted to them that he made his Cross an instrument of power by which the ultimate will of God could be done.[3]

And Dr. de Dietrich writes of this necessity:

[3] *The Will of God*, p. 48.

116

"The Son of man must suffer." This has nothing to do with the "fatalism" of ancient philosophy. This kind of necessity is something very different. It is based on who God is and who man is, on how intolerable God's holiness is to man, and how intolerable man's sin is to God.[4]

There were three basic choices facing Jesus as he saw the opposition grow and saw what result of his challenge lay ahead. The first was to compromise, to tone down his message, to soften his challenge, to be politic and careful, arguing (as so many of his followers have argued) that "more would be achieved in the long run by not pressuring people and stirring up opposition." This he rejected absolutely. He had come to call men, not to bargain with them. The second was to overwhelm them with power, to call in the "legions of angels" at his command and either force their submission or wipe them out. This, too, he rejected. He had come to win men, not to wipe them out. The third was to go ahead, doing the right with absolute certainty and openness, holy and obedient, hoping to the last that the appeal of holiness and love would win them, but prepared to die rather than give them up or separate himself from them.

So to the cross he went, not because his Father insisted on such a satisfaction but because the love of the

---

[4] *God's Unfolding Purpose,* p. 183.

Father which was also in him would not let him give us up. "Though they slay me, yet will I love them." The cross loomed not as God's demand for satisfaction but as the final dreadful extent to which human sin would go when faced with utter holiness. The terrible truth is that we tend to hate rather than love the better, because it "shows us up for what we are," and to kill rather than serve the best, because his holiness underscores our sinfulness. So, in a final outburst of rage in which we all have our part, men tried to escape the comparison between what they are and what they ought to be by killing God incarnate. This is the real atheism.

The cross was necessary because sin left no other way; the cross, as the place of suffering and death, is the work of sin, which is the cause of suffering and death. The refusal of man in pride and anger to submit to the holiness of Christ, to give up his arrogance and follow the Lord—this made the cross necessary and inevitable. The cross is firstly and originally the sign of sin and the work of evil. There can be nothing more evil than to take holiness and hurt it, to take love and hate it, to take God and kill him. To say that this, the summit of evil, is in origin the work and will of God is to distort truth. The cross is the work of man—sick, sinful, corrupt man. Jesus came to save all men, and they would not be saved. God's will was their salvation, and they rejected his will. It is the supreme example of evil.

9

THE ACTIVITY OF GOD

"Jesus went with them." Luke 24:15

The cross is the supreme example of evil, but it is much more; it is the supreme example of what we now examine in our next statement.

Statement Eleven. God is at work overcoming sin. Let us start this statement with two quotations, both of which are mistaken in their arguments, at opposite poles. Sigmund Freud writes of

that system of doctrines and pledges that on the one hand explains the riddle of this world to him with an enviable completeness, and on the other hand assures him that a solicitous Providence is watching over him and will make up to him in a future existence for any shortcomings in this life. The ordinary man cannot imagine this Providence in any other form but that of a greatly exalted father, for only such a one could understand the needs of the sons of men, or be softened by their prayers and placated by signs of their remorse. The whole thing is so patently infantile, so incongruous with reality, that to one whose attitude to humanity is friendly it is painful to him to think that the great majority of mortals will never be able to rise above this view of life.[1]

Now, by way of contrast, take this passage from Princess Mary's letter of sympathy to Julie on the death of her brother, in Tolstoy's *War and Peace:*

Your loss is so terrible that I can only explain it as a special providence of God, who, loving you, wishes to try you and your excellent mother. Oh, my friend! Religion, and religion alone, can—I will not say comfort us—but save us from despair. . . . Just as you ask destiny why your splendid brother had to die, so I asked why that angel Lise, who not only never wronged anyone, but in whose soul there were never any unkind thoughts, had to die. And what do you think, dear friend? Five years have passed since then, and already I, with my petty understanding, begin to see clearly why she had to die, and in

---

[1] Sigmund Freud, *Civilization and its Discontents,* Sec. 2.

what way that death was but an expression of the infinite goodness of the Creator, whose every action, though generally incomprehensible to us, is but a manifestation of His infinite love for His creatures. . . . His will is governed only by infinite love for us, and so whatever befalls us is for our good.[2]

They are both wrong and, as examples of their different lines of thought, they are not unrelated. The kind of faith expressed in Princess Mary's letter is enough to drive others, like Freud, away to the opposite extreme; rather than a God and Providence like this, they say, better no God at all. The letter is so typical of a strong tradition of Christian thought that it may well serve as an example. There is in it all the determinism, near to fatalism, with which we have been dealing through these statements. There is the "faith" which asks us to believe, for example, that the dear God kills off our loved ones "to try us." What a picture of love! On this basis, as we have seen, the obvious thing for Jesus to do was to let Jairus' daughter die, the widow of Nain's son be buried, and Lazarus lie in the tomb— to "try" their loving, sorrowing families. No wonder she says in her letter that religion can only save us from despair and not comfort us; and religion can only save us from despair by doing what Freud so despised, by

[2] Book 6, chap. 25.

121

making a "pie-in-the-sky" promise, the shortcomings and sorrows of this life, inflicted by God, being "made-up-for" in a future existence. No wonder, too, that when she forces herself to believe that the untimely death of a dear young life is "an expression of the infinite goodness of the Creator," she has to add that the Creator's actions are generally incomprehensible to us. On that basis I agree. Quite incomprehensible!

She is right to say that his will is governed only by infinite love for us; but is she right to say that "whatever befalls us is for our good"? Here we come to one of the major causes of confusion in thinking about the will of God. Take the particular instance in this letter. A dear, sweet person dies, to the grief and loss of her family and friends; five years later the writer looks back and sees that God has brought good out of the evil; God has been at work. She sees that by some miracle of his grace, God has overcome the evil. She then misguidedly says, "Good has come out of it, therefore it must not have been evil at all in the first instance." And she is *wrong*.

But just here is where so many go clear off the track in their thinking. Evil strikes; God overcomes it by bringing good out of it; so they argue, falsely, that it must not have been evil at all—it must have been his will all along! And when we so argue, we are wrong, for we are either denying the reality of evil or we are attributing it to God, accusing him of making the end justify the means. We are charging him with "doing wrong that good may come." The whole argument of this book has been against attributing anything sinful, hurtful, evil, to God. Infinite love, infinite holiness do not do what this letter attributes to him; it is not possible. If it is, as she says, "terrible," it is not his work; if it is his work, it cannot conceivably be called "terrible."

But God is at work. Wherever he is given the chance he overcomes evil with good, but that does not make the evil any less evil. Wherever he is given the chance he brings good out of bad, but the bad was still bad and was not caused by him. And of this, the cross is the supreme example; the cross was intended to be a thing of complete shame and defeat, utterly evil in its conception; God brought glory and victory out of it; but this does not alter one fraction the evil and wickedness of the intention behind the cross. Men intended Jesus to be finished forever, executed in disgrace and buried in dishonor; God turned it around and made out of it the sign of his victory and grace, to the honor of his name. This is God at work; this is he in whom we put our trust.

He will not do evil that good may come; but when evil is done, if he is given the opportunity in our lives, he will bring good out of it and thereby defeat evil. We

123

look back and say, *not* "It must have been his own work, even the seeming evil, because good has emerged from it." Rather we say, "God has brought good out of an inherently evil situation which was not of his making and has overcome evil with good in his holy power."

(Admittedly we may sometimes call something evil at the time it happens and on later reflection decide that it was not evil at all. We have all wanted and prayed for things we believed were good and felt hard hit when they never came, only to look back at some later time and realize that the worst thing for us would have been to have gotten what we wanted. This lies in the experience of us all, but while there may be some overlapping between the two, we are mostly very clear on the distinction between what was a mistaken wish and what was an evil event. Wanting some personal desire and wanting world peace in 1939 were two vastly different things; the failure of the first to materialize may have been a "hidden blessing"; the loss of the second was due to evil and to nothing but evil.)

God is at work, not causing grief in order to bring joy but bringing joy out of grief and so defeating the spirit of evil; not killing off our loved ones in order to try us but, even out of that "so sore loss," bringing new strength of character, new depth of compassion. Do not let the victory of his grace mislead you into thinking that he caused the pain or death over which he conquers; for as soon as you do that, it all becomes unreal, a puppet show. He knocks us down in order to pick us up; he hurts us in order to heal us; he kills our loved ones in order to "try us" and "make us better." It is all not too far removed from the story of the man who was asked why he went on banging his head against a wall and replied. "Because it feels so good when I stop." On much the same basis God, we are asked to believe, hurts and wounds us, so that we will feel so good when he quits! What a vision of God some of us present! What a travesty of the gospel! What a picture of life, cringing along wondering when God our Father is going to "clobber us for our own good," believing that he hurts and breaks our hearts to "try us"!

If it is evil, it is not his doing, but he is active in the situation to conquer evil, and he will if we will let him. If there is suffering, it is not his doing, but let him get at it, and out of it he will bring good and defeat the suffering. If there is death, it is the result of mankind's long sin, but watch what he does with it—he defeats it. He makes the cross into the sign of his triumph, and he makes our little human death into the gateway to immortal life, with him in his glory.

He is at work, not just conquering the sin and evil and suffering that happen but with us in constant, positive action for good. The word "Providence" has become so associated with the idea of the "frowning Providence," behind which he hides the "smiling face," that I hesitate to use it. "Providence" for many people brings the very idea I want to avoid—the idea of God "knocking us down in the incomprehensible mystery of his infinite love and goodness in order to pick us up again"—like Daddy smacking his child on the side of the head in order to be able to "kiss it and make it better."

I need a word that will express the fact that God is active not only in overcoming evil but in promoting and encouraging all good; that every influence of heaven is about us for our guidance and blessing; that he is trying, with every power he has (short of compelling us against the freedom he has given us), to lead us into the truth and joy and fullness of life. We must never feel that we walk helpless and unprotected, surrounded by unseen and unknown forces that may spring out on us without warning to beat us down, to wreck our joy. Instead we must feel that in a very real way "Jesus walks with us," that we walk in a creation in which every energy of the ultimate power is directed toward health and joy of body, mind, and soul. He is pouring out the energy of love—power goes forth from him to heal us all; he is knocking with urgent patience at the door to be let in and allowed to work in us; he is waiting and seeking every opportunity we will grant him to bring his good will about in us and in our world. He is working in and through every agency, seeking to overthrow sin and restore man to the health, the wholeness, that once was his. The research scientist who seeks a cure for cancer is working for God, because God—far from sending such pain—is working for the overthrow of all pain and suffering. The doctor who diagnoses and prescribes is a channel for God's energy; the surgeon who operates to restore health is in line with God's purpose; the counselor who seeks to heal the mind, who tries to

> minister to a mind diseas'd,
> Pluck from the memory a rooted sorrow,
> Raze out the written troubles of the brain,
> And with some sweet oblivious antidote
> Cleanse the stuff'd bosom of that perilous stuff
> Which weighs upon the heart,[3]

is aligning himself with the will of God; the social worker, the child-guidance counselor, the probation officer, the "senior citizen" visitor, the ordinary men and women who try in any way, in their homes, neighborhoods, businesses, and recreation, to help and forward truth and peace and health, in themselves and in others —these are all doing the will of God which is truth and peace and health and joy. Best by far, of course, if they

[3] William Shakespeare, *Macbeth,* Act 5, Sc. 3.

do it consciously, aware of him and of his power, calling on his help and committing their work to his service. The Christian doctor, counselor, social worker, and layman are channels for God's power in a way of special effectiveness, because they are aware of him as the source of health and joy; but unhappily so many Christians have such a strange view of God and his will that they block off much of their effectiveness as channels for his energy, for they cannot dare to believe what his will really is.

Job may be right, as a factual statement of man's life in this corrupt world, to say that "man is born for trouble as the sparks fly upward," but Father Zosimma is more deeply right, as the statement of God's intention for us, to say that "men were made for happiness." *This* is God's will.

So I do not feel that I walk through a world where I am a helpless victim of evil that may strike me down (though it may—an accident, a stroke, a heart attack— who knows when or where?), but walking in a world surrounded by the grace of God, with every power of heaven bent on me in love for my good, and the assurance that even if evil strikes, God will be able (if I let him) to bring good out of it. Still less do I feel that I walk in a world in which God himself is waiting around the corner to pounce on me and knock me down "for his glory and my good"; instead, he walks with me along the same road and shares with me my experiences and asks me to let him bring me good out of all of them. Nor do I feel, through my happiness, the pagan insecurity, shared by far too many Christians, that springs from the fear that, as Dryden's Cleopatra says, "The jealous Gods looked on my Joys with envious Eyes,"[4] for I do not feel that if I am "too happy" God will take it from me to "cut me down to size and keep me in my place." My happiness may go from me, through my own sin or some other external evil acting on me and my situation, but I know that God will want to defeat the sin and bring a new happiness out of the experience. For God is good and only good.

So I walk, not as certainly and steadily as I should but still not as one fearing what God may do to me, for he will do me only good; and if the world does me wrong, God, if I let him, will bring me good out of it. So, for the want of a better word, let us, instead of the Providence of God, think confidently and thankfully of the activity of God.

This is the faith of the saints and martyrs; this is the secret of their happiness. Only a few have sought suffering as if it were a good in itself. Only a few have wanted martyrdom for its own sake (for this is a perversion); the joy of the saints is in some small degree the same as

---

[4] John Dryden *All for Love*, Act 2.

the joy of the Lord—to be in his world, trying to make it more truly *his* world, trying to do his will; and if doing his will brings suffering, unpopularity, loss, or death itself, taking these things not as good in themselves, not as "sent by God," but as the inevitable result of trying to serve him in a corrupt world; as a privilege to be endured, not because they are good, but because they are suffered for his sake, as he endured the cross; and through it all, confident from faith and experience that out of it all he will bring good and blessing if we let him.

So now let us state the firm conclusions to which we are brought; let us outline the five main ways in which we touch and are touched in our lives, and see how we must look at them in our confidence in the absolute goodness of God. Let us for simplicity state them in terms of our own life; but as we do, we remember that what we say of ourselves applies to every other life—to our loved ones, to our friends, to every soul everywhere, known to us or unknown.

1. *If I choose good* (possible because we still have some little left of the original goodness he gave man), he increases its effect out of all proportion; and the glory is all his, for any good I have or do comes from him.

2. *If I mistakenly choose wrong,* thinking it to be good, he brings real good out of it. This touches on a problem we all face at times—plagued by uncertainty as

130

to which of two or more choices is the best. We thrash around and finally come to a reluctant decision, and then start "postmortems," wondering if we did right. Shouldn't we perhaps have done the other thing? Were we foolish in our choice? How we can torture ourselves! When faced with such a situation, let us think and pray about it as honestly and sincerely as we can; make our choice as truly and unselfishly as we can, seeking what is right in God's sight and then, having made our choice in that honest way, hand it over to God in the faith that, even if we did not choose the best, he will take it and bring good out of it. We have all seen so many torture themselves with futile regret, crying, "If only I had . . ." Certainly if they choose wrongly through selfishness or carelessness, regret is in order; but if they honestly made their choice as best they knew how, let them not torment themselves for being unable to foretell the future result. Rather let them trust that God takes our honest effort, even though it was mistaken, and uses it to bring good. From even the misguided and miscalculated he can bring blessing. But it would have been better still if we had chosen aright.

3. *If I suffer for my own sin* I know that the suffering comes from the sin, not from him, and that I alone am to blame; and I know that if I repent and ask, he will bring me to good through it. But it would have been far better if I had not sinned.

131

4. *If I suffer for the general sin of mankind over the centuries,* as part of our common humanity (and to which general sin I am a guilty contributor), it is not God who sends me the suffering or grief. It is still only the action and effect of sin. The result is a miracle —God bringing good out of evil. But it would have been better still if mankind had not sinned.

5. *If I suffer unjustly,* for my principles, for Christ's sake, it is not he who sends me the suffering. It is still only the work of evil; but he calls me to let him conquer it so that out of it he may bring good; of which the cross is the supreme example. But it would have been best if the world accepted good and loved it, rather than hated it and killed it.

As Teilhard de Chardin says:

I know that the powers of evil, considered in their deliberate and malign action, can do nothing to trouble the divine milieu around me. As they try to penetrate into my universe, their influence (if I have enough faith) suffers the lot common to all created energy; caught up and twisted round by Your irresistible energy, temptations and evils are converted into good and fan the fires of love.[5]

So, then, we must make a last statement.

Statement Twelve. The final word is his. We are not victims, not corks bobbing on the water, blown and beaten this way and that by forces beyond our compre-

[5] *The Divine Milieu,* p. 130.

hension. Nor are we finally victims even of the sin that lives in us and in our environment, for the last word is his and all that is foreign to him must disappear. We live in the knowledge of his absolute goodness; we live in the light with his hand upon us in love—the hand that never hurts, the hand that tries constantly and actively to lift us up if we have fallen by our own stumbling (because we would not let his hand lead us), or been tripped and knocked down by the sin of the world (because the world refused to let his hand lead it). The only thing that can defeat him is our own refusal to let him bless us; if we are willing, then out of every experience of life, even out of the evil and pain and grief which are not of his giving, he will bring wisdom, strength, character, and peace. Good and only good is what he gives.

So great is his power and his positive action for our blessing that even when the ultimate enemy strikes and we cry like Iras,

> Finish, good lady; the bright day is done,
> And we are for the dark,[6]

his hand leads us into the eternal light. The last, seeming victory of sin is turned into defeat, and out of the last blow of evil against us is brought good; and into that good night may we go gentle.

The final word is his.

[6] William Shakespeare, *Anthony and Cleopatra,* Act 5, Sc. 2.

10

THE SUMMARY OF THE ARGUMENT

This is the truth I saw then and still see,
Nor is there any magic that can stain
The white truth for me, or make me blind again.

EURIPIDES, HIPPOLYTUS [1]

Dmitri Karamazov speaks for many puzzled hearts when he says: "It's terrible what mysteries there are! Too many riddles weigh men down on earth. We must solve them as we can, and try to keep a dry skin in the water." Mysteries there are indeed, and on one of them we must touch before the close, for it is raised by the argument for man's real freedom. If man is truly free, and if the choice he makes is a real choice, how does

[1] Tr. by Gilbert Murray (London: Allen & Unwin Ltd., 1902), p. 23, lines 388-90.

this freedom relate to God's omniscience? If God knows everything, knows exactly and precisely what my choice will be, is my freedom of choice real? It is not enough to say that he "knows" my choice as I "know" that a child, offered a choice between candy and bitter medicine, will certainly choose the candy; for though I know it with some certainty, there is no absolute certainty, and there is a real though distant possibility that the child may prove me wrong by choosing the medicine. God cannot be "proved wrong" in this way. When we say that he "knows," it is in the absolute sense of complete and certain knowledge. He knows what you will choose, what you will do; and he knows it as a fact, not just as a probability. If then your future actions are already known to him absolutely, is your choice real?

This is a mystery and will remain essentially a mystery. It was this same mystery that prompted the psalmist to cry:

> Even before a word is on my tongue,
>> lo, O Lord, thou knowest it altogether.
> Thou dost beset me behind and before,
>> and layest thy hand upon me.
> Such knowledge is too wonderful for me;
>> it is high, I cannot attain it. (Ps. 139:4-6.)

It will remain too high for us to attain, but there are

some pointers that may help us at least to "keep a dry skin in the water."

1. We tend, guard against it as we may, to transfer our human experience to our thinking about God. We talk of his "fore-knowing" a future which is only "future" to us and not to him. We are "in time" and we stream along from the past through the present into the future; and the events of our life stream from the future through the present into the past. It is all that we know in this life, and because it is all that we know, we assume too easily that it is all that is to be known— that the life to come will be similar in structure to this, that there will be a time sequence stretched out to infinity. Eternal life is thought of as "everlasting" life— going on and on; and by that very word we try to insinuate the time sequence of our mortal world into the eternity of God. It is, of course, this concept of "never-ending" life that makes many people unsure of its desirability. "Just to go on and on forever and ever," they say. "Who wants it?" Actually, *they* want it, in preference to being blotted out—as with physical death in this life, it is easy to say that you do not want to live forever, as long as you are alive. If faced by the choice the vast majority would take even "endlessness" in preference to oblivion. Nevertheless, the reaction is real and true in that a mere extension of time to infinity seems a poor

kind of heaven. There is a genuine feeling of dismay at the prospect of endlessness by itself.

Eternal life must be thought of as a life so different in quality that the concept of time, of events stretching from "back there" on to "way out there," is so inadequate as to be meaningless. We must assume that in God's eternity the familiar distinctions of past, present, and future are superseded, and that the quality of life, not its endlessness, is the completely dominant fact. We may even find a faint foreshadowing of the difference in our present experience. We all have instances in our experience when time seemed endless; we were bored, or waiting for something to happen or someone to come; we waited for what seemed to us, in our curiously thoughtless phrase, "an eternity," but when we next looked at our watch, only a few minutes had crawled past. Time weighed oppressively on us, and because the quality of life was low, time seemed endless; and we even felt, perhaps, that hell might be simply unending time, unfilled by any real quality of life. Then, at the opposite extreme, we know instances when we were immersed in joyful activity, in meaningful touch with our fellowman, in rich enjoyment of life's blessings, and then we cried out about how quickly the hours had gone. They seemed like fleeting moments; we had hardly been aware of time at all, and our one regret was to be brought back to an awareness of time's passing;

and we even knew, with a strange joy, that in heaven there is no "time," no past, present, future as we know them now—no long string of endless events, but a life of such quality that time can have no meaning.

At best, and it is a poor best, this can only be a foreshadowing of something beyond our grasp, but even a foreshadowing (or, better, a forelightening) may help us to avoid thinking of God and omniscience in terms of time sequence and the mere passage of events. As his Scots mentor says in C. S. Lewis' book: "Do not fash yourself with such questions. Ye cannot fully understand the relations of choice and time till you are beyond both." [2]

2. The second and most significant clue is in the life of Christ. He came out of eternity into the world of our experience, the world of space and time; he lived in our spatial, time-related conditions, and in those conditions he dealt with men and women as with people having a real, genuine, and meaningful freedom of choice. Nowhere can you find him dealing with people as if with those whose fate is already decided, whose future actions are not merely known to God but determined by God. Further, he talks of himself, within this time structure, as having options, freedom of decision and choice; in simple matters—"With what can

[2] *The Great Divorce*, pp. 65-66.

138

we compare the Kingdom of God, or what parable shall we use for it?"—as one picking and choosing between the possible choices of illustration; and in the gravest matter, praying that he might be spared the cross, as one facing a real possibility that there might be some other way. His life and teaching do not solve the problem for us, for he kept silent about it; but they do force us not only to accept the fact of the mystery but to insist that we are right in saying, "Even if this is a mystery, we still say that man is really free, by God's decision, although what he chooses is known to God." But if we add "before man makes the choice," we are again in danger of putting God into time. It can only be left as mystery, but before we leave it, let us remember that there are one or two strange incidents in which Jesus mixed up his tenses deliberately. He "confuses" past, present, and future tenses in a way that we would not dare to do, and would not know how to do. One in particular is so strange, so pregnant with meaning, that when we think on it it may send a tingle of awareness through us. "Before Abraham was, I am." (John 8:58.) And there we must leave the mystery until we understand fully, even as we have been fully understood.

So now let us summarize the whole argument of this book in the twelve statements that have been made.

1. *The world in its origin is God's creation* and was, therefore, in its origin entirely good. There was no sin, no suffering, no pain, no tears, no death.

2. *God created man in his own image.* Man in God's intention was a being pure, sinless, obedient, but also free; not a puppet—a man.

3. *Man is a fallen creature.* He abused, and continues to abuse, his God-given freedom and rebelled against God, and so brought suffering and death into his life.

4. *Nature has been corrupted along with, or by, man's sin.* Nature, too, knows suffering and death, contrary to God's original purpose.

5. *Suffering, pain, and death are evil.* They were not in God's original plan, nor are they to be found in his final purpose, for they are to be banished from the "new heaven and earth."

6. *All suffering is due to sin.* The corruption of mankind infects us all and we are part of it, sometimes suffering for our own, sometimes for mankind's rebellion, sin working out in pain and death in beings intended for joy and life.

7. *Man's free will is impaired by his sin but not destroyed.* Some of the goodness God originally gave man

lingers still; he cannot save himself, but he can want the good he cannot achieve (and this is part of his torment), and he can respond to God's offer in Christ of salvation (which is the answer to his torment). It is a real though small freedom, a real choice, and a real responsibility for the choice.

8. *All men are elect and called.* God's appeal is to all, and his desire is that all should repent and come to him and be saved. Jesus said, "It is not the will of my Father who is in heaven that one of these little ones should perish" (Matt. 18:14).

9. *God is made known in Christ.* In Jesus of Nazareth we see God and can speak with confidence about his will, because we see it revealed in the life and action, the death and resurrection of our Lord. God is not inscrutable; his will is not incomprehensible, because Christ has revealed him to us.

10. *Christ came into the world to save all men.* He came primarily to save not to die. His offer of salvation was made genuinely and freely to all men who were (and are) free to accept or reject him; and when they rejected him, he accepted the cross, not as an end in itself but because there was no other way for perfect love to take.

141

11. *God is at work overcoming sin.* The cross which was meant to be defeat was transformed into victory. So through all life we find God overturning evil; not causing it but overthrowing it; not sending it but conquering it. So that. . .

12. *The final word is his.* Not sin but God is the ultimate word, and the worst that sin can do can be defeated and good brought about. This is the faith in which we stand; and we look to the day when nature will regain her lost good, when "God will wipe away every tear from their eyes," and as at the beginning so at the end with Christ, "Death shall be no more, neither shall there be mourning nor crying nor pain any more" (Rev. 21:4).

None of us knows what tomorrow may hold; but we know that it holds the good God, whose love is more active and personal than we are ready to believe; not a vague benevolence but a direct, positive force, the ultimate power in the universe, which can turn even disaster into a means of blessing and death's strict arrest into the perfect liberty of eternal life, which can blunt every thrust of evil against us, and which will not let us go, for we are his; each and all of us—his.

INDEX

143

God can and will—if given the oppor tunity—bring good out of it and thereb defeat evil.

Good God! Cry or Credo? takes to tasl the "Christian fatalism" so often found in those who have suffered injury or loss It presents questions to challenge sucl thinking, and will lead to a belief in God more consistent with what the New Testament tells us. This book should foster more open discussion of this problem, breaking it wide open for many good people who have remained quiet about their doubts and for many ministers who have avoided a frank study of the problem.

THE AUTHOR

HUBERT BLACK, a native of Edinburgh, Scotland, is now minister of Franklin Street Presbyterian Church Baltimore, Maryland.

Mr. Black attended Edinburgh University (M.A.) and New College in Scotland and then studied at Union Theological Seminary in New York (S.T.M.). He served churches in Scotland from 1940 until 1958, when he came to the United States as minister of Highland Presbyterian Church, Fayetteville, North Carolina. He remained there until 1964.